The Neomycins and
Related Antibiotics

E. R. SQUIBB LECTURES ON

Presented at the Institute of Microbiology
Rutgers, the State University of New Jersey

F. H. Stodola, *Chemical Transformations
      by Microorganisms*, 1957

V. H. Cheldelin, *Metabolic Pathways
      in Microorganisms*, 1960

K. Hofmann, *Fatty Acid Metabolism
      in Microorganisms*, 1962

K. L. Rinehart, Jr., *The Neomycins
      and Related Antibiotics*, 1961

Herbert E. Carter

CHEMISTRY OF MICROBIAL PRODUCTS

The Neomycins and Related Antibiotics

By **KENNETH L. RINEHART, Jr.**
Associate Professor of Organic Chemistry
University of Illinois

NEW YORK · LONDON · SYDNEY, JOHN WILEY & SONS, INC.

In recognition of the importance of cooperation between chemist and microbiologist the E. R. Squibb Lectures on Chemistry of Microbial Products were established with the support of The Squibb Institute for Medical Research in 1955. The lectures are presented annually in the fall at the Institute of Microbiology, Rutgers, the State University of New Jersey, New Brunswick, New Jersey.

PREFACE

The present small book on the chemistry of neomycin and related amino sugar antibiotics has been taken rather loosely from the series of three lectures on the subject presented at the Institute of Microbiology, Rutgers, in mid-December of 1961. In the months since then much has happened in neomycin chemistry, and these latest results have been incorporated where appropriate; it is especially satisfying to be able now to write final formulas for neomycins B and C and to include some results in agreement with the general biosynthetic scheme proposed at the time of the lectures. From January to September 1962 I was the happy holder of a Guggenheim Fellowship, and much of the actual writing of the monograph was accomplished in Zürich and Stockholm and aboard the *Cristoforo Colombo*. Indeed, some of the newer methods which have helped to complete the structures have developed from discussions with colleagues abroad during those months.

In the fourteen years since the discovery of the neomycins chemical research on them has passed from an initial phase of frenetic activity, largely in industrial laboratories, in which the general nature of the molecule was established, into a more leisurely phase, largely in universities, in which the complex stereochemistry has been deciphered. It is to the latter phase that our efforts at the University of Illinois belong. As an earlier author (D8) wrote, "It was, therefore, rather tacitly accepted, when the similar, complex nature of neomycin became apparent, that the pursuit of the ultimate structural features of the molecule, crossing the *t*'s and dotting the *i*'s as it were, would remain of academic interest only." This dotting the *i*'s and crossing the *t*'s has consumed over seven years for us now and has occupied the attention of six graduate students, three postdoctoral fellows, and one determined undergraduate girl. It is a particular pleasure to be able to discuss here our studies which have led to the elucidation of the structures of the neomycins, the first carbohydrate antibiotics to be known in complete stereochemical detail.

Certainly the credit for the neomycin structures goes to my coworkers, who have labored faithfully through Urbana summers of 100% humidity, with milligram quantities of hygroscopic materials: Doctors Peter Woo, Alexander Argoudelis, Townley Culbertson, Klaus Striegler, Martin Hichens, James Foght, and Scott Chilton; Messrs. Robert Johnson and Richard Schimbor; and Mrs. Karen Rover Sandberg. I should also like here to express my appreciation to Doctor Thomas Eble of the Upjohn Company for very generous samples of neomycins B and C; to the United States Public Health Service for grants in support of the neomycin work; and especially to Professor Herbert E.

Carter, for arranging our first gift of neomycin and providing throughout our studies a wealth of background, insight, and advice.

K. L. RINEHART

Urbana, Illinois
November, 1963

CONTENTS

The Neomycins and
Related Antibiotics

INTRODUCTION

Recent years have seen the introduction of so many new antibiotics that it now seems remarkable an antibiotic could still be called neomycin or the "new mycin" in 1949. At the time of its discovery by Waksman and Lechevalier (W1), however, not many other antibiotics were known—penicillin, tyrothricin, the actinomycins, streptomycin, bacitracin, polymyxin, chloramphenicol, streptothricin, chlortetracycline, grisein, and a few others. Neomycin showed considerable therapeutic promise in its early days, and it was not until somewhat later that its nephrotoxic and ototoxic properties (H1) were recognized. Still, even today, it is one of the more effective antibiotics against many organisms, and it is widely used in presurgical bowel cleansing (M1) and for topical applications (L1).

THE NEOMYCIN COMPLEX

Shortly after its discovery, neomycin was recognized to consist, in fact, of more than one isomeric substance, and the name neomycin complex was coined to include these materials. Neomycins A, B, and C were reported to be separated by countercurrent distribution (S1, S2), but this method was subsequently reported to be unsatisfactory for effecting good separation (S3). Neomycins B and C have, however, been separated by chromatography over alumina (D1) and over charcoal (F1). Of these procedures charcoal chromatography is undoubtedly the most successful in effecting complete separation, and, by utilizing a larger ratio of charcoal to antibiotic than that reported by earlier workers, Chilton recently has been able to effect separation of four different neomycin components in one mixture (C1). Still better separation is effected by chromatography of the N-acetyl derivatives of the neomycins over cellulose (P1, R1), but it has not yet proved possible to regenerate the unacetylated neomycins from their N-acetyl derivatives.

The compound originally described as neomycin A (P2) was subsequently recognized as a fragment of both neomycins B and C rather than a true neomycin. Its identity with the neamine of Leach and Teeters (L2) and the methanolysis fragment A of Dutcher et al. (D1) was established by two independent sets of investigators (L3, D2). The question whether neamine exists as such in the fermentation broth or arises as an artifact from acid hydrolysis during neomycin isolation has been of considerable interest. Evidence would seem to favor the former viewpoint, since under some growing conditions neamine may actually become the favored product of fermentation (P3). In addition, recent studies of the incorporation of labeled glucose into neomycin indicate that neamine production is, to a degree, independent of that of neobiosamine, the second fragment of the intact neomycin molecule (R2, R3). Lastly, no evidence has thus far been presented for the presence of neobiosamine in the neomycin complex isolated.

The isomeric neomycins isolated, neomycins B and C,

were shown initially to differ in rotation and in biological activity, as seen in Table 1.1. The relative activities of neomycins B and C indicated in Table 1.1 represent an extreme example (S4); neomycin B was more active than neomycin C against most of the organisms tested, but the difference was frequently slight (S4). Neomycin preparations sold commercially are actually mixtures of the two components standardized to prescribed activity and consisting usually of 85–90% neomycin B.

The molecular formula of neomycins B and C ($C_{23}H_{46}N_6O_{13}$) shows them to be isomeric, and the chemical difference between them has been a point of considerable interest due to the difference in activity of the two compounds. Studies directed toward elucidation of the structures of neomycins B and C have been conducted at a number of laboratories—at the Institute of Microbiology, Rutgers University; at Merck and Company; at the Squibb Institute for Medical Research; at Chas. Pfizer and Company; at The Upjohn Company; and at the University of Illinois—over the last thirteen years. From these studies it is now possible to derive the structures for neomycins B and C presented in Chapter 4.

TABLE 1.1

Properties of Neomycins B and C

	Neomycin B	Neomycin C	Ref.
	$C_{23}H_{46}N_6O_{13}$	$C_{23}H_{46}N_6O_{13}$	(R4)
$[\alpha]_D^{25}$	$+83°$	$+121°$	(F1)
Activity *	1 μg./ml.	250 μg./ml.	(S4)

* Amount of antibiotic needed to inhibit growth of *Sarcina lutea*, ATCC 9341, or a *Corynebacterium* species.

METHANOLYSIS OF NEOMYCINS B AND C

Although the molecules are exceedingly complex, their chemistry is reasonably divided into portions. On mild methanolysis neomycin B is cleaved to give two fragments, neamine and the methyl glycoside of neobiosamine B (D1), as shown in Fig. 1.1. Similar methanolysis of neomycin C gives neamine, identical to the material isolated from neomycin B, and methyl neobiosaminide C, differing from the isomeric product from neomycin B (D1). The chemistry of the fragment common to both neomycins—neamine—is discussed at length in Chapter 3, whereas Chapter 2 deals with the chemistry of the neobiosamines, the fragments which differ in the two neomycins. Chapter 4 discusses the glycosidic linkages and the structures of the intact neomycins, and Chapter 5 the structures of antibiotics closely related to the neomycins. Finally, consideration is given to biosynthesis of the neomycins in Chapter 6.

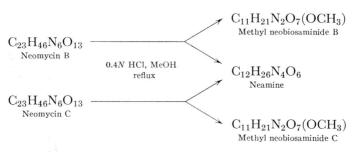

$C_{23}H_{46}N_6O_{13}$
Neomycin B

$C_{23}H_{46}N_6O_{13}$
Neomycin C

0.4N HCl, MeOH
reflux

$C_{11}H_{21}N_2O_7(OCH_3)$
Methyl neobiosaminide B

$C_{12}H_{26}N_4O_6$
Neamine

$C_{11}H_{21}N_2O_7(OCH_3)$
Methyl neobiosaminide C

Fig. 1.1. Dutcher et al. (D1), Ford et al. (F1).

2

THE CHEMISTRY
OF THE NEOBIOSAMINES

THE METHYL NEOBIOSAMINIDES

At the end of Chapter 1 it was noted that methanolysis of neomycin B produces, together with neamine, the methyl glycoside of neobiosamine B, whereas the corresponding methanolysis of neomycin C gives neamine and methyl neobiosaminide C (Fig. 1.1). In fact, these compounds were obtained pure only after chromatography over charcoal (R1, R5). Specific rotations of chromatographic eluants of fractions containing methyl neobiosaminides B and C are shown in Figs. 2.1 and 2.2, respectively. In each chromatogram early fractions (e.g., a and b) contain some unreacted neomycin and neamine, whereas later fractions (c, d, and e) contain only the methyl neobiosaminides. Methanolysis would be expected to produce both the α- and β-anomers of the glycosides, and this is, indeed, the case. In each chromatographic run the rotation of the methyl neobiosaminide obtained steadily decreased in successive fractions, indicating a shift from preponderantly α- to largely β-glycoside. That these were, in fact, glycosidic isomers was

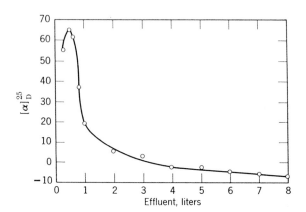

Fig. 2.1. Argoudelis (R1).

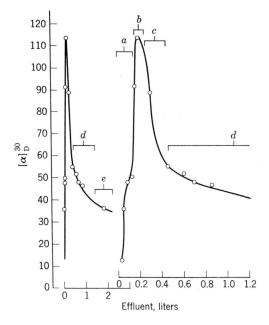

Fig. 2.2. Woo (R5).

6

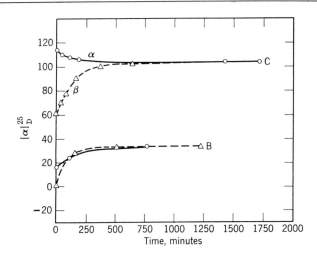

Fig. 2.3. Woo (R5).

demonstrated by mild hydrolysis of several fractions of each run to give neobiosamines B and C of the same specific rotation from the α- and β-glycosides; this is seen in Fig. 2.3. Properties of the isomeric neobiosamines and of their methyl glycosides are summarized in Table 2.1.

TABLE 2.1

Properties of Neobiosamines and Methyl Neobiosaminides

	$[\alpha]_D^{25}$	Mol. Formula
Neobiosamine B	$+33°$	$C_{11}H_{22}N_2O_8$
C	$+104°$	
Methyl neobiosaminide B (α)	$+13°$	$C_{11}H_{21}N_2O_7(OCH_3)$
B (β)	$-17°$	
C (α)	$+113°$	
C (β)	$+61°$	

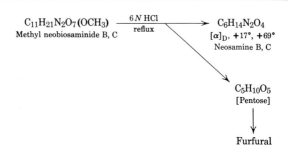

Fig. 2.4. Dutcher et al. (D1), Woo and Argoudelis (R6).

The neobiosamines may readily be shown to be disaccharides. On vigorous acid hydrolysis (D1) methyl neobiosaminide B gives neosamine B (R6), a diaminohexose (R4), together with furfural, which may be presumed to arise from degradation of a pentose also formed in the hydrolysis. Similarly, vigorous hydrolysis (D1) of methyl neobiosaminide C gives a diaminohexose, neosamine C (R6), isomeric with neosamine B, and furfural. These results and the optical properties of the isomeric neosamines are summarized in Fig. 2.4. Neobiosamines B and C are thus disaccharides of a pentose (which will be shown later to be the same in the two neobiosamines) and diaminohexoses neosamines B and C (R4).

D-RIBOSE

It was noted above that vigorous acid hydrolysis of the methyl neobiosaminides gave degradation of the pentose obtained; mild hydrolysis was unsuccessful in cleaving the bond between the pentose and the neosamine. Such resistance to hydrolysis is characteristic of glycosides of amino sugars and has been most thoroughly studied for glycosides of glucosamine (K2). It is undoubtedly due to electrostatic shielding of the glycosidic bond by an ammonium group in its vicinity. Normal glycoside hydrolysis proceeds by protonation of the glycosidic oxygen, as shown in Fig. 2.5, and this step is inhibited when the glycoside is proximate to a basic group, as shown in Fig. 2.6. To circumvent this difficulty it is necessary to remove the basic group. The simplest method of effecting this is acylation to give a neutral amide. Hydrolysis then may take two alternative paths, as shown in Fig. 2.7; either the glycosidic bond or the amide bond may be cleaved first, to give a free sugar or the free amine, respectively.

In the case of methyl neobiosaminide C (R7) the free

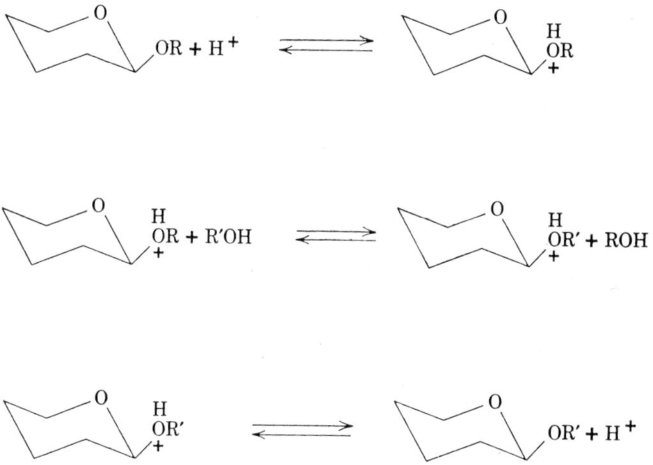

Fig. 2.5

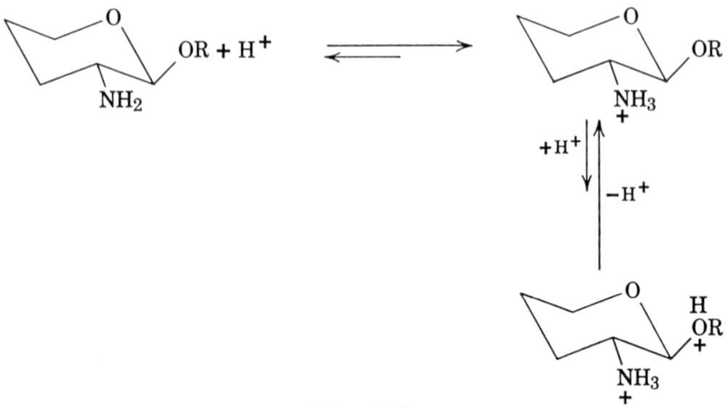

Fig. 2.6

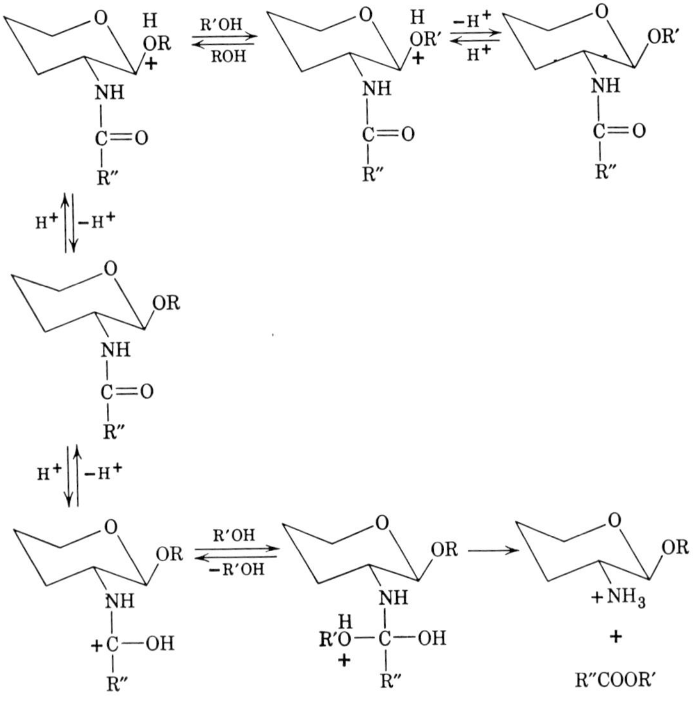

Fig. 2.7

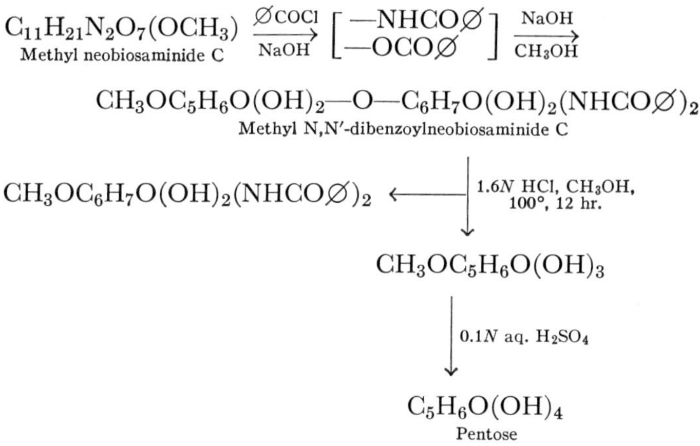

$\underset{\text{Methyl neobiosaminide C}}{C_{11}H_{21}N_2O_7(OCH_3)} \xrightarrow[\text{NaOH}]{\varnothing\text{COCl}} \left[\begin{array}{l} -\text{NHCO}\varnothing \\ -\text{OCO}\varnothing \end{array}\right] \xrightarrow[\text{CH}_3\text{OH}]{\text{NaOH}}$

$$\underset{\text{Methyl N,N'-dibenzoylneobiosaminide C}}{CH_3OC_5H_6O(OH)_2\text{—}O\text{—}C_6H_7O(OH)_2(\text{NHCO}\varnothing)_2}$$

$$CH_3OC_6H_7O(OH)_2(\text{NHCO}\varnothing)_2 \longleftarrow \underset{100°, \text{ 12 hr.}}{\overset{1.6N \text{ HCl, CH}_3\text{OH,}}{\Big\downarrow}}$$

$$CH_3OC_5H_6O(OH)_3$$

$$\Big\downarrow \; 0.1N \text{ aq. H}_2\text{SO}_4$$

$$\underset{\text{Pentose}}{C_5H_6O(OH)_4}$$

Fig. 2.8. Woo (R7).

amino groups were converted to the benzamido derivatives by polybenzoylation in base under Schotten-Baumann conditions, then removing the O-benzoate by selective saponification of the ester groups. Mild hydrolysis of methyl N,N'-dibenzoylneobiosaminide C then gave in good yield the free pentose, as shown in Fig. 2.8.

Similarly, the amino groups of methyl neobiosaminide B were protected by benzoylation, and hydrolysis of methyl N,N',O-tribenzoylneobiosaminide B also gave the pentose (R7), as shown in Fig. 2.9. Alternative methods (Fig. 2.9) of eliminating the basic amino groups involved their removal by treatment with periodate (R9) or with nitrous acid (R1). Each of these treatments was followed by hydrolysis to give the free pentose.

From both methyl neobiosaminides B and C the pentose isolated on hydrolysis was shown to be D-ribose (R7). Its

$CH_3OC_5H_6O(OH)_2—O—C_6H_7O(OH)_2(NH_2)_2$

Methyl neobiosaminide B

$$\xrightarrow[\text{(2) NaOH}]{\text{(1) } \varnothing COCl} R—(NHCO\varnothing)_2$$

$$\xrightarrow{\text{NaIO}_4} \quad NH_3\uparrow \quad \xrightarrow[80-100°]{1N \text{ HCl}} \text{Pentose}$$

$$\xrightarrow[\text{HOAc}]{\text{AgNO}_2} \quad N_2\uparrow$$

Fig. 2.9. Argoudelis (R1), Chilton (R9).

phenylosazone formed mosslike clumps (ribosazone) rather than needles (xylosazone), it gave color reactions typical of aldopentoses rather than of ketopentoses, and it was most conclusively identified as ribose by means of paper chromatography in a number of solvent systems (Table 2.2). Finally, its rotation was negative, establishing the D-configuration.

TABLE 2.2

R_F Values of Pentoses

Solvent	Ribose [d]	Arabinose [d]	Xylose [d]	Lyxose [d]	Hydrolysate B [d]	Hydrolysate C [d]
BAW [a]	0.368(5)	0.317(4)	0.333(4)	0.341(5)	0.362	0.364(6)
PhNC [b]	0.630(3)	0.545	0.470	0.554(2)	0.625	0.630(2)
BAW [c]	0.596(3)	0.537(2)	0.542(2)	0.546(3)	0.598(3)	

[a] n-BuOH:HOAc:H_2O = 4:1:5.
[b] Phenol + 1% NH_3 + HCN.
[c] t-BuOH:HOAc:H_2O = 2:2:1.
[d] The number of runs averaged is in parentheses.

It is possible for the neosamine moiety of neobiosamine to be attached to ribose by a glycosidic bond involving the carbonyl group of either of the two fragments. A neosaminido-ribose is *per se* more likely, since the glycosidic bond from neobiosamine to neamine in neomycin and to the methyl group in methyl neobiosaminide is cleaved readily by acid (suggesting a riboside) while the glycosidic bond within neobiosamine is stable to acid hydrolysis (suggesting a neosaminide). This was established rigorously for both neobiosamines B and C. In the latter case (R8) neobiosamine C was reduced to neobiosaminol C with sodium borohydride, then converted to the N,N'-dibenzoyl derivative (Fig. 2.10). Hydrolysis of this gave ribitol rather than ribose, showing the presence of the free ribose carbonyl in neobiosamine C. Data already presented establish neobiosamine B, too, as a neosaminido-ribose (see Fig. 2.9). It will be recalled that hydrolysis of periodate-oxidized methyl neobiosaminide B gave ribose (R9). This would have been impossible had the compound been a ribosido-neosamine since then, regardless of whether the ribose were in the

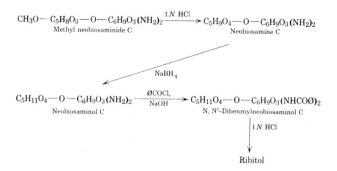

Fig. 2.10. Woo (R8).

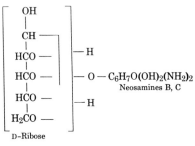

Neobiosamines B, C

Fig. 2.11

furanose or pyranose form, a vicinal glycol group would be required in ribose, allowing its destruction by periodate. Another method has been employed by Van Stolk et al. (V4) to show the free ribose carbonyl in neobiosamine, involving the sequence

Neomycin → methyl neobiosaminide →

neobiosamine $\xrightarrow{\text{H}^+}$ furfural

When, however, neobiosamine was oxidized first with hypoiodite, then hydrolyzed, no furfural was obtained. From the results presented thus far, the structures of the neobiosamines could be represented by Fig. 2.11.

NEOSAMINE C

The structure of neosamine C, the diaminohexose fragment of neobiosamine C, was established (R6) largely by identification of degradation fragments obtained from periodate oxidation of derivatives of neosamine C. Accordingly, it is perhaps appropriate to review briefly the molecular groupings (Fig. 2.12) which are normally cleaved by periodate. This subject has been reviewed more extensively elsewhere, of course (D4). The vicinal glycol function is the group most readily and reliably attacked by periodate; if one of the hydroxyl groups is primary, then formalde-

$$
\begin{array}{c}
\overset{|}{-\mathrm{C}-\mathrm{OH}} \\
\overset{|}{-\mathrm{C}-\mathrm{OH}} \\
|
\end{array}
+ \mathrm{IO_4^-} \rightleftarrows
\begin{array}{c}
\overset{|}{-\mathrm{C}-\mathrm{O}} \\
\diagdown \\
\overset{|}{} \quad \mathrm{IO_3^-} \\
\diagup \\
\overset{|}{-\mathrm{C}-\mathrm{O}} \\
|
\end{array}
\rightarrow
\begin{array}{c}
\overset{|}{-\mathrm{C}{=}\mathrm{O}} \\
+ \\
-\mathrm{C}{=}\mathrm{O} \\
|
\end{array}
+ \mathrm{IO_3^-}
$$

$$
\begin{array}{c}
\overset{|}{-\mathrm{C}-\mathrm{OH}} \\
\overset{|}{-\mathrm{C}-\mathrm{OH}} \\
\overset{|}{-\mathrm{C}-\mathrm{OH}} \\
|
\end{array}
\xrightarrow{\mathrm{IO_4^-}}
\begin{array}{c}
\overset{|}{-\mathrm{C}{=}\mathrm{O}} \\
+ \\
-\mathrm{COOH} \\
+ \\
-\mathrm{C}{=}\mathrm{O} \\
|
\end{array}
$$

$$
\begin{array}{c}
\overset{|}{-\mathrm{C}-\mathrm{OH}} \\
\overset{|}{-\mathrm{C}-\mathrm{NH_2}} \\
|
\end{array}
\xrightarrow{\mathrm{IO_4^-}}
\begin{array}{c}
\overset{|}{-\mathrm{C}{=}\mathrm{O}} \\
+ \\
-\mathrm{C}{=}\mathrm{O} \\
|
\end{array}
+ \mathrm{NH_3}
$$

$$
\begin{array}{c}
\overset{|}{-\mathrm{C}-\mathrm{OH}} \\
\overset{|}{-\mathrm{C}-\mathrm{OR,}} \\
|
\end{array}
\quad
\begin{array}{c}
\overset{|}{-\mathrm{C}-\mathrm{OH}} \\
\overset{|}{-\mathrm{C}-\mathrm{OCOR,}} \\
|
\end{array}
\quad
\begin{array}{c}
\overset{|}{-\mathrm{C}-\mathrm{OH}} \\
\overset{|}{-\mathrm{C}-\mathrm{NHCOR}} \\
|
\end{array}
\xrightarrow{\mathrm{IO_4^-}}
\begin{array}{c}
\mathrm{No} \\
\mathrm{reac\text{-}} \\
\mathrm{tion}
\end{array}
$$

R = alkyl, aryl

Fig. 2.12

hyde is obtained, whereas a secondary hydroxyl gives another aldehyde and a tertiary hydroxyl a ketone. A 1,2,3-triol system takes up 2 moles of periodate, giving two carbonyl compounds and 1 mole of acid. Replacement of the hydroxyl group by an amino group does not alter the periodate uptake pattern beyond giving a mole of ammonia for each primary amino group attacked. It is usually assumed that a hydroxyl group may be protected by conversion to an ether or an ester grouping and that an amino group may be protected by conversion to an amide, although this latter assumption may be questioned; see (R8) and (R12).

Neosamine C was converted by sodium borohydride to neosaminol C, and from this the N,N'-dibenzoyl derivative was prepared (R6). This derivative consumed 2 moles of periodate, but gave no formaldehyde. The product mixture (presumably containing the aldehydes shown in Fig. 2.13) was oxidized with bromine water and subsequently hydrolyzed with hydrochloric acid. Analytical paper chromatography revealed the presence of glycine and serine. The latter amino acid was identified as L-serine by comparison of the rotation of the periodate oxidation mixture with that obtained from periodate oxidation of N-benzoyl-D-glucosaminol. This result establishes the stereochemistry at C-2 as the same as that in D-glucosamine (i.e., on the right in the Fischer projection formula).

Methyl N,N'-dibenzoylneobiosaminide C was found to consume 2 moles of periodate (Fig. 2.13). Again, bromine water oxidation converted the aldehydes obtained to acids; subsequent hydrolysis in this case gave glycine and isoserine, identified by analytical paper chromatography. Preparative paper chromatography and extraction of the isoserine spot

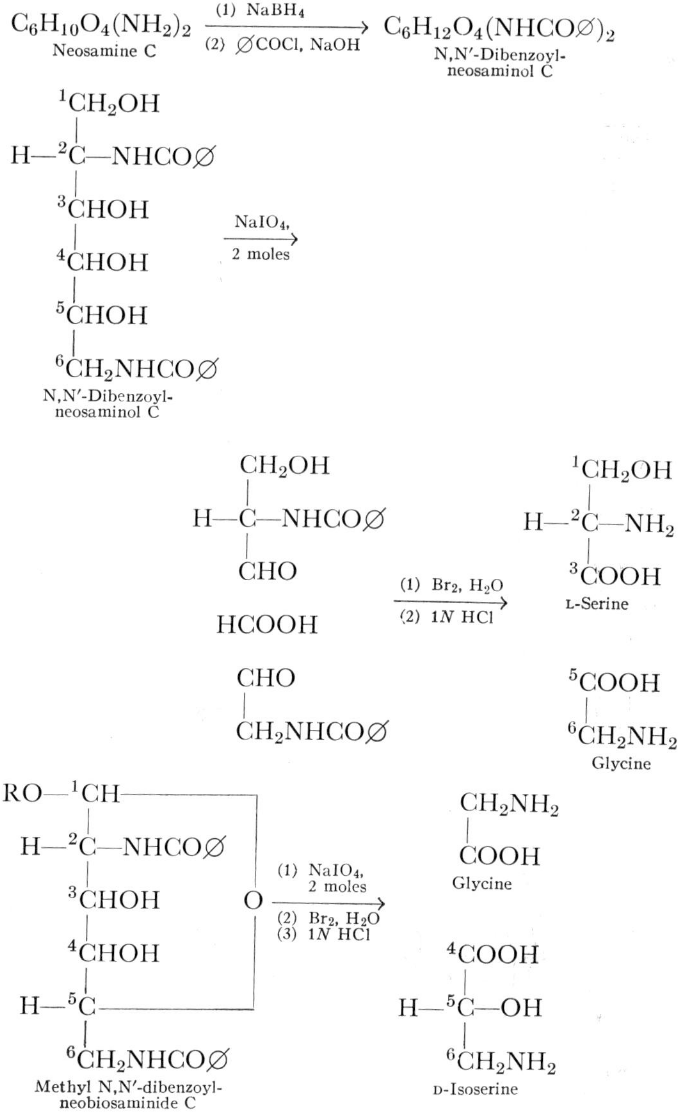

$$C_6H_{10}O_4(NH_2)_2 \xrightarrow[\text{(2) } \emptyset COCl,\ NaOH]{\text{(1) } NaBH_4} C_6H_{12}O_4(NHCO\emptyset)_2$$

Neosamine C N,N′-Dibenzoyl-neosaminol C

```
 ¹CH₂OH
   |
H—²C—NHCO∅
   |
 ³CHOH          NaIO₄,
   |          ─────────→
 ⁴CHOH          2 moles
   |
 ⁵CHOH
   |
 ⁶CH₂NHCO∅
```

N,N′-Dibenzoyl-
neosaminol C

```
 CH₂OH                              ¹CH₂OH
   |                                   |
H—C—NHCO∅                          H—²C—NH₂
   |                                   |
 CHO              (1) Br₂, H₂O       ³COOH
               ───────────────→     L-Serine
 HCOOH            (2) 1N HCl

 CHO                                ⁵COOH
   |                                   |
 CH₂NHCO∅                           ⁶CH₂NH₂
                                    Glycine
```

```
RO—¹CH─────┐                        CH₂NH₂
   |       │                           |
H—²C—NHCO∅ │       (1) NaIO₄,        COOH
   |       │          2 moles        Glycine
 ³CHOH     │O ───────────────→
   |       │       (2) Br₂, H₂O      ⁴COOH
 ⁴CHOH     │       (3) 1N HCl          |
   |       │                        H—⁵C—OH
H—⁵C───────┘                           |
   |                                 ⁶CH₂NH₂
 ⁶CH₂NHCO∅                          D-Isoserine
```

Methyl N,N′-dibenzoyl-
neobiosaminide C

Fig. 2.13. Woo (R6).

gave material of positive rotation, establishing the D-con-figuration of the isoserine and assigning neosamine C to the D-hexose series.

Since the stereochemistry at C-2 and C-5 was established by these experiments, only four possibilities existed for the diaminohexose neosamine C (i.e., D-gluco-, D-galacto-, D-gulo-, or D-allo- stereochemistry; see Fig. 2.14). Kuhn and his co-workers have shown that the aminohexoses have rotations very similar to those of the corresponding hexoses (K4), i.e., the replacement of a hydroxyl group by an amino group has little effect on the rotation of the compound, a result expected from Brewster's correlations of group rotations (B1). On this basis, both D-allo- and D-gulo- stereochemistry may be eliminated, since D-allose and D-gulose (and their cor-

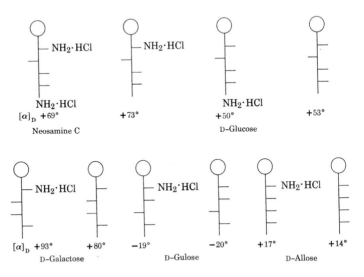

Fig. 2.14. Kuhn et al. (K4).

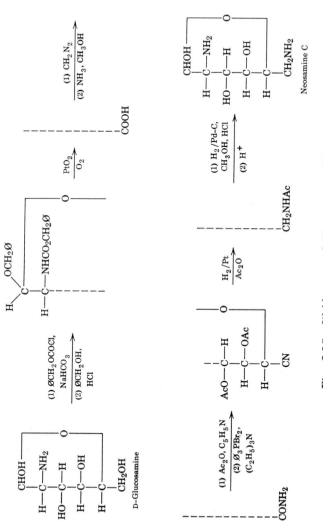

Fig. 2.15. Weidmann and Zimmerman (W4).

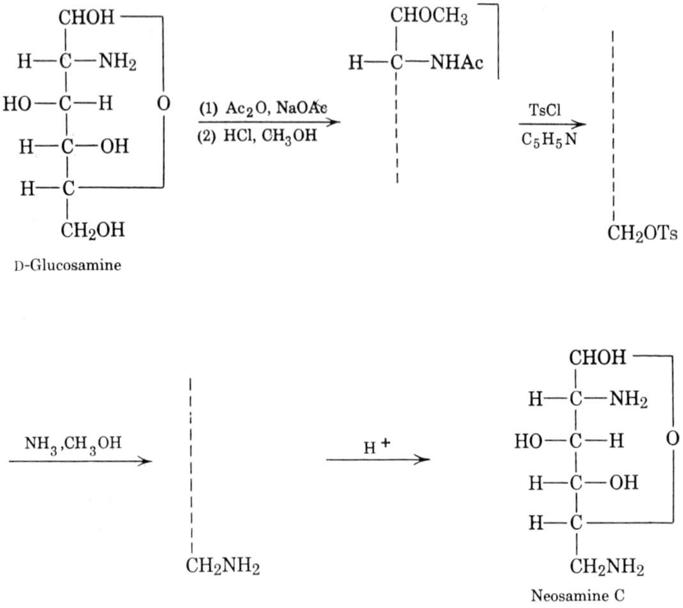

Fig. 2.16. Culbertson and Rover (R10).

responding 2-deoxy-2-amino derivatives) have rotations of $-20°$ $(-19°)$ and $+14°$ $(+17°)$, respectively, as shown in Fig. 2.14.

The remaining two possibilities, D-glucose and D-galactose, both have rotations reasonably near that of neosamine C; however, D-glucose is clearly much preferred, since the rotation of D-glucosamine is nearly identical to that of neosamine C. In this respect it may be noted that replacement of a 2-hydroxyl group by an amino group increases rotation somewhat, but that replacement of a 6-hydroxyl group by an amino group (at least in D-glucose) has essentially no effect on the rotation. Thus, the rotation of neosamine C should approximate that of its 2-hexosamine parent.

Neosamine C then was assigned the structure 2,6-diamino-2,6-dideoxy-D-glucose. This has recently been confirmed by syntheses in two laboratories. That of Weidmann and Zimmerman (W4) is summarized in Fig. 2.15 and that of the Illinois group (R10) in Fig. 2.16. In either synthesis the asymmetric centers are not affected, since transformations are effected at C-1 and C-6 only. The yields in the two routes are roughly equivalent, but the route of Fig. 2.15 requires approximately four steps more. The products from both syntheses were shown to be identical to neosamine C by rotations and R_F values of the three sugars and by rotations, melting points, and nuclear magnetic resonance (n.m.r.) spectra of their N-acetyl derivatives (Table 2.3).

The linkage of neosamine C to ribose was assigned the α-configuration from Hudson's rules of isorotation (R6). Although strict application of Hudson's rules was impossible since no authentic α- or β-derivatives of neosamine were known, the high positive rotation of neobiosamine C com-

TABLE 2.3

Properties of N,N'-Diacetylneosamine C (R10)

	Melting Point	$[\alpha]_D$	R_{NAG}
N,N'-Diacetylneosamine C [a]	209–215°	35.6°	1.33 [c]
"N,N'-Diacetyldiaminohexose II" [b]	211–216°	37.2°	1.32
Synthetic (Rover, Culbertson)	207–212°	35.8°	1.32
Synthetic (Weidmann, Zimmerman)	209–213°	36.8°	1.32

[a] From neomycin.
[b] From zygomycin AII.
[c] R_F compared to N-acetyl-glucosamine.

TABLE 2.4

Molecular Rotations

	$[M]_D$
D-Ribose	$-3,450$
Neosamine C	$+17,100$
Neobiosamine C	$+32,200$

pared to the molecular rotations of neosamine C and of ribose allowed assignment of the α-configuration (see Table 2.4). This was supported (R6) by an infrared band at 844 cm^{-1}, in a region characteristic of α-linkages, and recently has been confirmed (R11) by the small coupling constant, $J_{12} = 2.6$ c.p.s., of the H_1-H_2 protons of neosamine C in the neobiosamine portion of N-hexaacetylneomycin C. In the C1 chair conformation such small coupling indicates an *ae, ea,* or *ee* H_1-H_2 relationship (L5, P5), or *cis* in the present case.

NEOBIOSAMINE C

The position of attachment of neosamine C to D-ribose was originally assigned (R8) at C-2, since it was felt that all other possible positions had been eliminated, as outlined in Fig. 2.17. A C-3 attachment was considered eliminated by the 2-mole periodate uptake of methyl N,N'-dibenzoyl-neobiosaminide C. Since only 1 mole could have been consumed in the neosamine C portion of the molecule, the other mole, it was reasoned, must have been consumed by the ribose; thus, the requirement of a vicinal glycol grouping in ribose eliminated a glycoside linked at C-3, regardless of whether the ribose was furanose or pyranose. (Actu-

Ribose linkage

(a) *Not at* C-3:

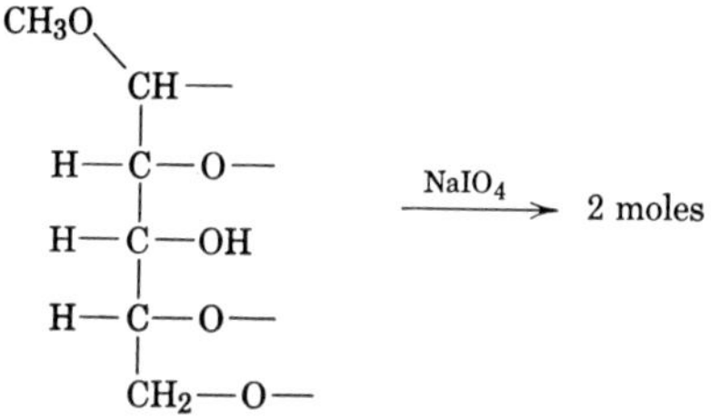

Methyl N, N'- dibenzoylneobiosaminide C

(b) *Not at* C-5:

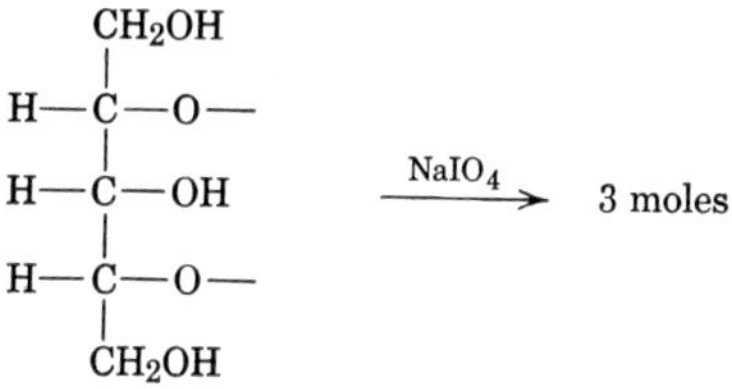

N, N'-Dibenzoylneobiosaminol C

(c) *Not at* C-4:

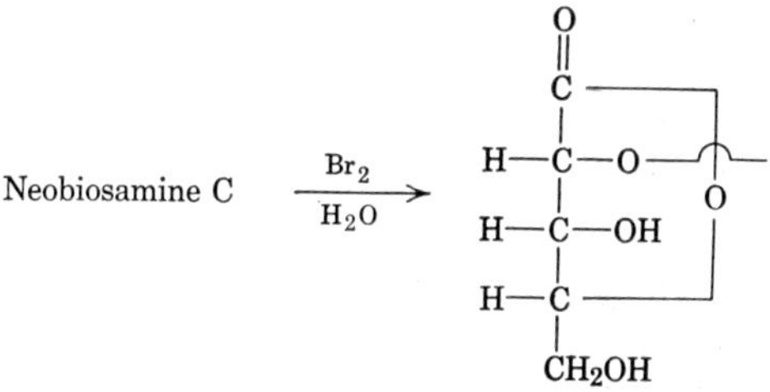

IR: 1765 cm^{-1}

(d) *Therefore: at* C-2

Fig. 2.17.   Woo (R8).

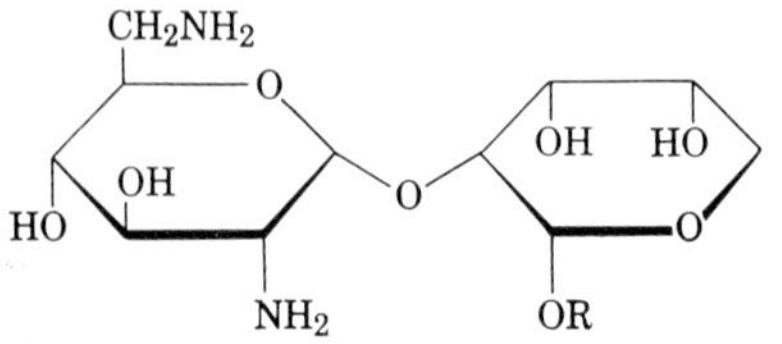

Neobiosamine C: R = H
Methyl neobiosaminide C: R = CH$_3$

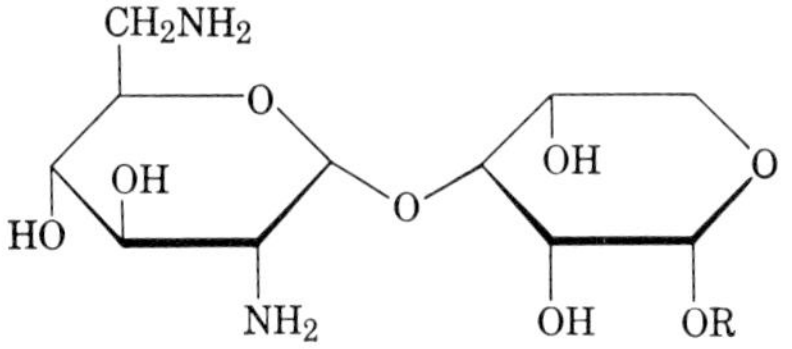

Fig. 2.18. Woo (R8), Chilton and Hichens (R9)

ally, it will be seen in Chapter 4 that neosamine C is, indeed, attached at C-3 of ribose and the periodate uptake data for methyl N,N'-dibenzoylneobiosaminide C is somehow anomalous.) A C-4 linkage was eliminated by the oxidation of neobiosamine C with bromine water; this gave a product with infrared absorption at 1765 cm^{-1}, characteristic of a γ-lactone, and established a free C-4 hydroxyl group. A C-5 attachment was eliminated by the observation that N,N'-dibenzoylneobiosaminol C consumed 3 moles of periodate rather than the 4 required for a C-5 attachment. The correct structure [derived later (R9)] and the incorrect structure for methyl neobiosaminide C are both presented in Fig. 2.18.[1]

---

[1] Actually the pyranose-furanose form of methyl neobiosaminide C has not been established. It is written here as pyranose, however, by

NEOSAMINE B

The structural elucidation of neosamine B paralleled closely that already presented for neosamine C (R12). Neo-

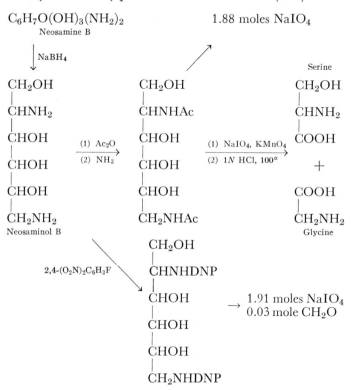

$$C_6H_7O(OH)_3(NH_2)_2 \qquad\qquad 1.88 \text{ moles } NaIO_4$$
Neosamine B

Fig. 2.19. Argoudelis (R12).

———

analogy to the established linkage in methyl neobiosaminide B (see Fig. 2.27).

samine B was reduced with sodium borohydride to neosaminol B, and this in turn was converted to its N,N'-di-
acetyl and N,N'-*bis*-(2,4-dinitrophenyl) derivatives. Each
of these derivatives consumed 2 moles of periodate, and no
formaldehyde was obtained (see Fig. 2.19). The acetyl derivative was subjected to periodate-permanganate oxidation,
then to hydrolysis; a papergram revealed the presence of
serine and glycine.

It is of interest here to note that periodate oxidation was
also employed to establish the fact that neosamine B is an
aldohexose, rather than a ketohexose. The free diaminohexose rapidly consumed 2 moles of periodate, but even
after 2.56 moles uptake, only 0.02 mole of formaldehyde
was found. A ketohexose structure should have given much
more formaldehyde (Fig. 2.20).

As with neosamine C, the stereochemistry at C-2 was established (R12) by comparison of the products obtained on

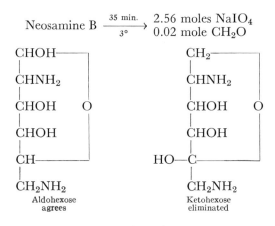

Fig. 2.20. Argoudelis (R12).

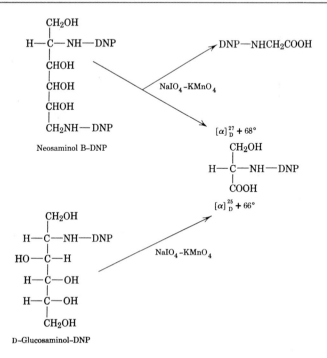

Fig. 2.21. Argoudelis (R12).

periodate oxidation of the corresponding derivative of D-glucosaminol, in this case its DNP derivative. From the identity of these products the amino group at C-2 must then be on the right in the Fischer projection formula of neosamine B, as in neosamine C (Fig. 2.21).

Periodate oxidation of methyl neobiosaminide B consumed 2 moles of periodate rapidly; then the product was converted to the DNP derivative and hydrolyzed (A2). A DNP derivative, presumably of isoserinaldehyde, was thus

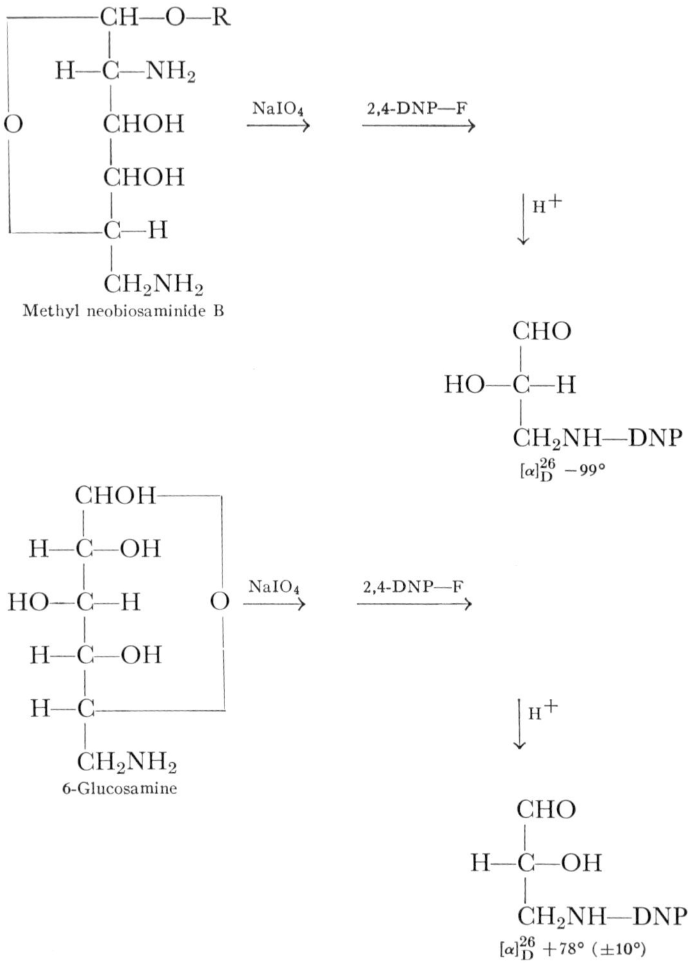

$$\begin{array}{c} \text{—CH—O—R} \\ | \\ \text{H—C—NH}_2 \\ | \\ \text{O} \quad \text{CHOH} \\ | \\ \text{CHOH} \\ | \\ \text{—C—H} \\ | \\ \text{CH}_2\text{NH}_2 \end{array}$$

Methyl neobiosaminide B

$\xrightarrow{\text{NaIO}_4}$ $\xrightarrow{\text{2,4-DNP—F}}$

$\Big\downarrow \text{H}^+$

$$\begin{array}{c} \text{CHO} \\ | \\ \text{HO—C—H} \\ | \\ \text{CH}_2\text{NH—DNP} \end{array}$$

$[\alpha]_D^{26} -99°$

$$\begin{array}{c} \text{CHOH} \\ | \\ \text{H—C—OH} \\ | \\ \text{HO—C—H} \quad \text{O} \\ | \\ \text{H—C—OH} \\ | \\ \text{H—C—} \\ | \\ \text{CH}_2\text{NH}_2 \end{array}$$

6-Glucosamine

$\xrightarrow{\text{NaIO}_4}$ $\xrightarrow{\text{2,4-DNP—F}}$

$\Big\downarrow \text{H}^+$

$$\begin{array}{c} \text{CHO} \\ | \\ \text{H—C—OH} \\ | \\ \text{CH}_2\text{NH—DNP} \end{array}$$

$[\alpha]_D^{26} +78° \ (\pm 10°)$

Fig. 2.22. Argoudelis (A2).

obtained, having a strong negative rotation ($-99°$). Corresponding periodate oxidation, subsequent dinitrophenylation, and hydrolysis of 6-amino-6-deoxy-D-glucose gave another DNP derivative, presumably of D-isoserinaldehyde, with a strongly positive rotation ($+78°$). The strongly negative rotation of the DNP derivative from neosamine B thus defines the stereochemistry at C-5 in neosamine B as that with the hydroxyl group on the left in the Fischer projection formula; i.e., the compound is of the L-hexose series (Fig. 2.22).

One cannot employ rotational arguments similar to those employed for neosamine C to establish the configuration of the remaining neosamine B asymmetric centers, since neosamine B and the four possible related amino sugars all have similar rotations (see Fig. 2.23). Fortunately, the curious behavior toward periodate of the dinitrophenyl derivatives of neosamine B eliminates two of the possibilities (L-altro and L-talo stereochemistry). Neither *bis*-2,4-dinitrophenyl-neosamine B nor *bis*-2,4-dinitrophenyl-neobiosamine B nor methyl *bis*-2,4-dinitrophenyl-neobiosaminide B consumes periodate. It might initially be assumed that the bulky DNP group protects the hydroxyl group adjacent to it simply by shielding it from periodate attack. This, however, appears not to be the case, since the corresponding DNP derivatives of neosamine C and of methyl neobiosaminide C are both attacked readily by periodate.

To explain the lack of periodate uptake by neosamine B derivatives, then, one must invoke conformational arguments. The DNP derivatives of neosamine B must exist in a conformation in which the two vicinal hydroxyl groups are further removed from one another than 60°, the dihedral angle subtended by the hydroxyl groups about the C-3, C-4 bond in neosamine C in the C1 chair conformation

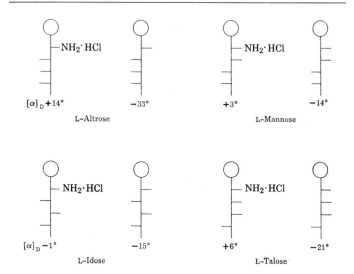

Fig. 2.23. Rotations estimated from values for D-isomers. Kuhn et al. (K4).

(see Fig. 2.24). If the two hydroxyl groups were on the same side of the ring in neosamine B (both right or both left in the Fischer projection formula), then they could not be further removed than 60° from one another regardless of whether the ring existed in a chair or a boat conformation. Thus L-talo and L-altro configurations (with *cis* C-3, C-4 hydroxyls) are both eliminated. Of the two remaining configurations, those of L-idose and L-mannose, it is impossible to choose one or the other on the basis of periodate evidence. There are conformations for each in which the dihedral angle subtended by the C-3, C-4 hydroxyls exceeds 60°. Some of these are shown for the L-ido configuration in Fig. 2.24. Somewhat arbitrarily, but in light of the

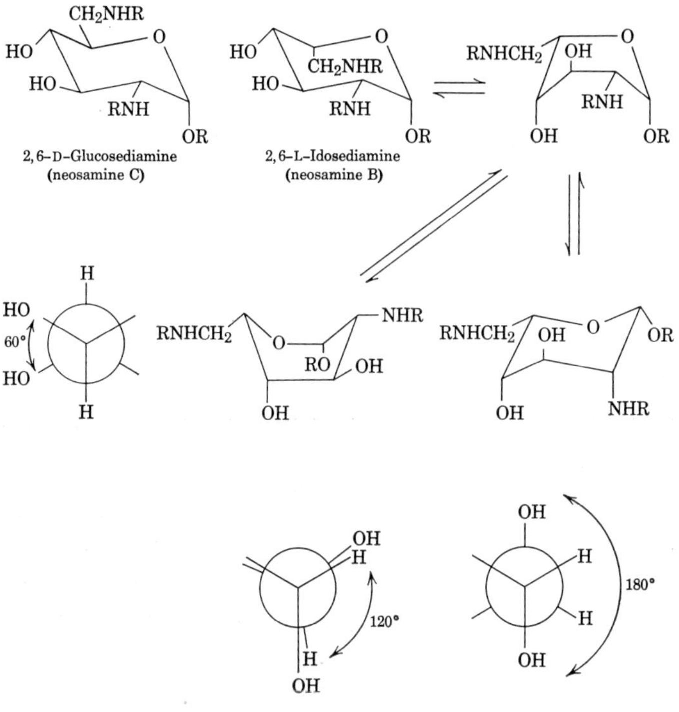

Fig. 2.24

biogenetic considerations presented in Chapter 6, and employing a "principle of minimum differentiation," the stereochemistry has been suggested to be that of L-idose (R9), since that configuration differs from D-glucose only by inversion at C-5.

It is of some interest to compare the electrophoretic behaviors of diacetylneosamines B and C; they differ considerably, as seen in Table 2.5. Migration in borate is frequently

TABLE 2.5

Electrophoresis Data

Compound	M_G	Ref.
N,N'-Diacetylneosamine C	0.24 [a]	(H8)
B	0.55	(H8)
N-Acetylglucosamine	0.33	(H8)
	0.23	(F2)
N-Acetylgalactosamine	0.35	(F2)
2-O-Methylglucose	0.23	(F2)
2-O-Methylgalactose	0.32	(F2)

[a] Migration relative to glucose, in $0.1M$ borate buffer.

indicative of one or more *cis* vicinal glycol groups, as may be seen from the comparative electrophoretic migrations of N-acetylglucosamine and N-acetylgalactosamine, and of 2-O-methylglucose and 2-O-methylgalactose, and of certain inositols (Table 3.2). A *cis* glycol grouping would, of course, indicate L-talo or L-altro stereochemistry and contradict the negative periodate data. Neither line of reasoning is completely conclusive, however.

The linkage between neosamine B and ribose in neobiosamine B may be assigned the same absolute configuration as that in neobiosamine C, from the high positive rotational increment (Table 2.6) in going to neobiosamine B

TABLE 2.6

Molecular Rotations

	$[M]_D$
D-Ribose	$-3,500$
Neosamine B	$+4,300$
Neobiosamine B	$+10,700$

from neosamine B (R11). Under strict Hudson nomenclature this would be the β-configuration for an L-sugar, but since the absolute configuration is the same as in neobiosamine C it is referred to here as an α'-configuration. This assignment of absolute configuration has recently been confirmed (R11) by the small coupling constant, $J_{12} = 1.6$ c.p.s., of the H_1-H_2 protons of neosamine B in N-hexaacetylneomycin B and other neosamine B derivatives, indicating the *cis* H_1-H_2 relationship.

NEOBIOSAMINE B

The 2-mole periodate uptake of methyl neobiosaminide B without formaldehyde formation (R12) establishes a pyranose form for neosamine B and at the same time limits the position of attachment of neosamine B to ribose to either C-2 (furanose) or C-3 (furanose or pyranose), since in either case ribose would not be attacked (Fig. 2.25). This was confirmed by papergrams which showed the presence of ribose even after a greater than 2-mole uptake of periodate.

The position was decided by methylation studies (R12). Methyl N,N'-diacetylneobiosaminide B was treated with barium oxide and methyl iodide to give the fully methylated derivative. After hydrolysis a neutral reducing material was obtained from a preparative papergram (Fig. 2.26). This compound did not react with periodate or migrate in a borate buffer system in paper electrophoresis, a result that establishes the absence of vicinal hydroxyl groups and narrows its structural choice to 2,4- or 2,5-O,O'-dimethylribose. This dimethylribose also gave R_F values corresponding to those previously reported for 2,4- and 2,5-dimethylriboses

Methyl neobiosaminide B $\xrightarrow[\text{0.05 mole CH}_2\text{O}]{\text{40 min. \quad 1.98 moles NaIO}_4}$

$$
\begin{array}{l}
\text{RO} - \text{CH} -\! \\
\quad\quad\; | \\
\quad\quad \text{CHNH}_2 \\
\quad\quad\; | \\
\quad\quad \text{CHOH} \quad\quad \text{O} \\
\quad\quad\; | \\
\quad\quad \text{CHOH} \\
\quad\quad\; | \\
\quad\quad \text{CH} -\! \\
\quad\quad\; | \\
\quad\quad \text{CH}_2\text{NH}_2
\end{array}
$$

where R =

$$
\begin{array}{l}
\text{CH}_3\text{O} - \text{CH} \\
\quad\quad\quad\; | \\
\text{H} - \text{C} \\
\quad\quad\; | \\
\text{H} - \text{C} - \text{OH} \quad \text{O} \\
\quad\quad\; | \\
\text{H} - \text{C} \\
\quad\quad\; | \\
\quad\quad \text{CH}_2\text{OH}
\end{array}
\quad \text{or} \quad
\begin{array}{l}
\text{CH}_3\text{O} - \text{CH} \\
\quad\quad\quad\; | \\
\text{H} - \text{C} - \text{OH} \quad \text{O} \\
\quad\quad\; | \\
\text{H} - \text{C} \\
\quad\quad\; | \\
\text{H} - \text{C} \\
\quad\quad\; | \\
\quad\quad \text{CH}_2\text{OH}
\end{array}
\quad \text{or}
$$

$$
\begin{array}{l}
\text{CH}_3\text{O} - \text{CH} \\
\quad\quad\quad\; | \\
\text{H} - \text{C} - \text{OH} \quad \text{O} \\
\quad\quad\; | \\
\text{H} - \text{C} \\
\quad\quad\; | \\
\text{H} - \text{C} - \text{OH} \\
\quad\quad\; | \\
\quad\quad \text{CH}_2
\end{array}
$$

Fig. 2.25. Argoudelis and Chilton (R12).

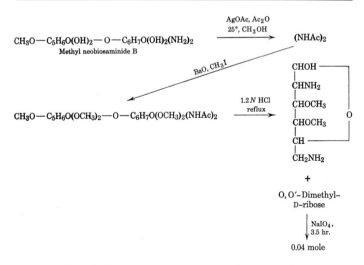

Fig. 2.26. Culbertson, Striegler, Chilton (R12).

(Table 4.1). On reduction the compound gave a nonreducing material. That the latter did not consume periodate or migrate in a borate buffer eliminated the 2,5-dimethyl-

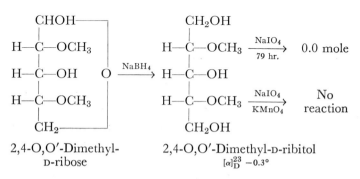

Fig. 2.27. Culbertson, Striegler, Chilton (R12).

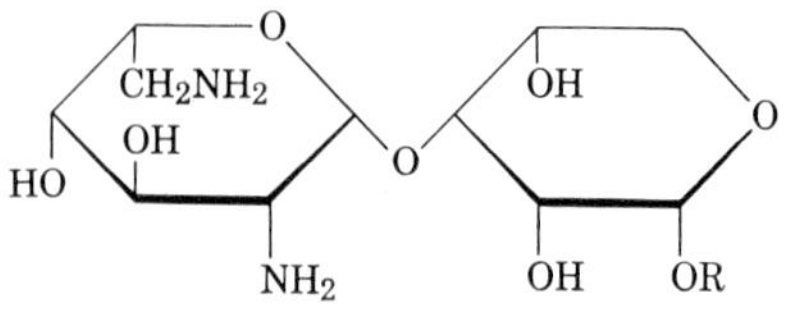

Neobiosamine B: R = H
Methyl neobiosaminide B: R = CH$_3$

Fig. 2.28

ribitol possibility, narrowing the choice to 2,4-dimethyl-ribitol. These results are summarized in Fig. 2.27.

In methyl neobiosaminide B, then, ribose is found in the pyranose form, and the structure assigned the former compound is that of Fig. 2.28. It should be noted, however, that although the pyranose form was thus established for methyl neobiosaminide B this result does not show the form of ribose in the intact neomycin. The latter point is discussed in Chapter 4.

ADDENDUM

The structure proposed earlier (R9) for neosamine B, 2,6-diamino-2,6-dideoxy-L-idose, has now been confirmed by three independent pathways.

In the first of these, Chilton (C12, R17) treated neosamine B with o-phenylenediamine to give the quinoxaline shown (Fig. 2.29), whose optical rotatory dispersion curve showed a negative Cotton effect and was nearly superimposable on that of the corresponding quinoxalines from neosamine C and D-glucose. This establishes the stereochemistry of

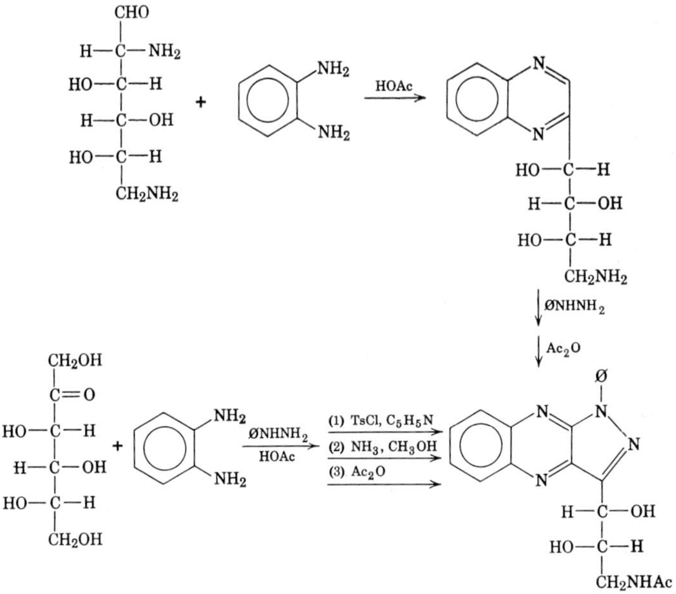

Fig. 2.29. Chilton (C12, R17).

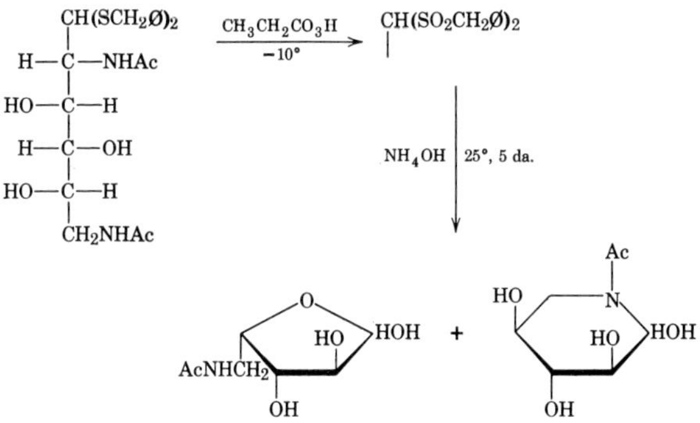

Fig. 2.30. Haskell and Hanessian (H19).

neosamine B at C-3 as the same as that of D-glucose. The quinoxaline from neosamine B was then converted to the phenylflavazole and this compound was synthesized from L-sorbose by the route outlined in Fig. 2.29.

Haskell and Hanessian (H19) have also obtained evidence assigning L-idose stereochemistry to neosamine B (paromose). Their degradative route is shown in Fig. 2.30. The mixture of 5-acetamido-5-deoxy-L-xylofuranose and 5-acetamido-

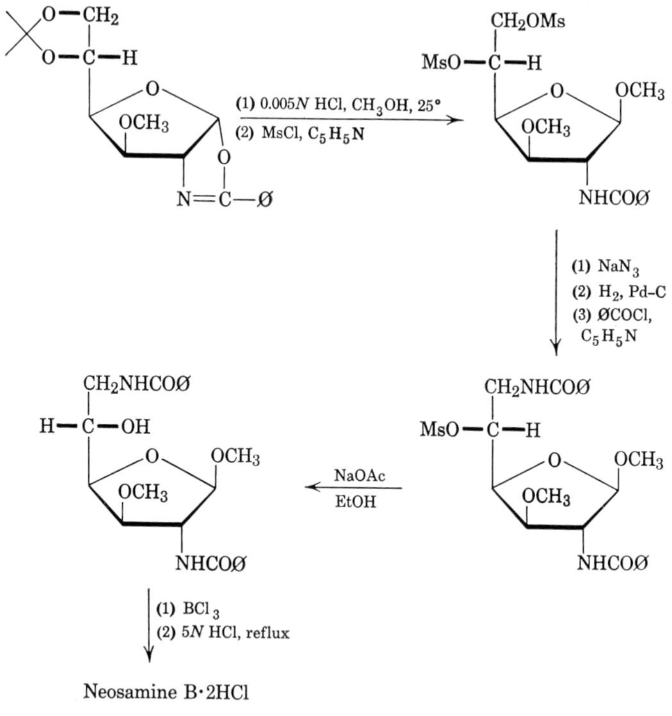

Fig. 2.31. Reckendorf (R18).

5-deoxy-L-xyloazapyranose formed by removal of C-1 of neosamine B was compared to the corresponding mixture of isomers of synthetic 5-acetamido-5-deoxy-D-xylose.

Reckendorf (R18) has reported the synthesis of 2,6-diamino-2,6-dideoxy-L-idose by the route shown in Fig. 2.31 and has indicated the product to be identical with neosamine B.

3

THE CHEMISTRY OF NEAMINE

HYDROLYSIS OF NEAMINE

It will be recalled from Chapter 1 that mild acidic methanolysis of both neomycins B and C gives neamine, a fragment common to both. Neamine itself has mild antibiotic activity against certain microorganisms (S4) and is one of only a very few degradation products of antibiotics which have been shown to have this property. It is a nonreducing material and is exceedingly resistant to acidic hydrolysis, a property for which its four primary amino groups are responsible (see Table 3.1).

TABLE 3.1

Properties of Neamine (L2)

Reported Values

Physical	$[\alpha]_D^{22}$ +123°	m.p. 256° dec.
Spectral	UV: blank 212–360 mμ	IR: no C=O
Chemical	$C_{12}H_{26}N_4O_6$ 4NH$_2$	no O—CH$_3$, N—CH$_3$,
	or C—CH$_3$	
Antibacterial	250 μg./ml.[a]	

[a] Activity against organisms of Table 1.1.

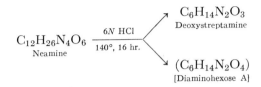

Fig. 3.1. Kuehl, Bishop, and Folkers (K1), Dyer (D3).

On very vigorous acid hydrolysis (48% hydrobromic acid, 12N hydrochloric acid, etc.), however, neamine is cleaved (K1, D3) into two equivalent portions (see Fig. 3.1). One of the fragments of this hydrolysis is deoxystreptamine, a compound completely stable to acids. The other fragment, however, is decomposed under these conditions and has not been isolated from this reaction.

DEOXYSTREPTAMINE

Deoxystreptamine was the first of the fragments of the neomycins to yield to structural elucidation, through the work of Kuehl, Bishop, and Folkers (K1). The intact molecule consumed 4 moles of periodate, establishing that all hydroxyl or amino groups were vicinal. On the other hand, the N,N'-dibenzoyl derivative consumed only 2 moles of periodate, indicating that the three hydroxyl groups must be vicinal to one another and the amino groups at the end of this system (Fig. 3.2). The 2-mole periodate product (dialdehyde, Fig. 3.3) was converted to the dithioacetal which, in turn, was reduced over Raney nickel to *meso*-2,4-dibenzamidopentane, a compound synthesized by way of the authentic route shown (Fig. 3.3). Thus deoxystrep-

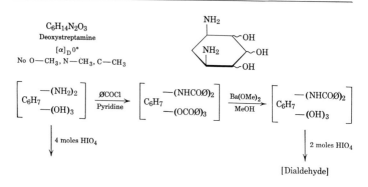

$C_6H_{14}N_2O_3$
Deoxystreptamine
$[\alpha]_D \, 0°$
No O—CH$_3$, N—CH$_3$, C—CH$_3$

$$\left[C_6H_7 \begin{matrix} -(NH_2)_2 \\ -(OH)_3 \end{matrix} \right] \xrightarrow[\text{Pyridine}]{\text{ØCOCl}} \left[C_6H_7 \begin{matrix} -(NHCOØ)_2 \\ -(OCOØ)_3 \end{matrix} \right] \xrightarrow[\text{MeOH}]{\text{Ba(OMe)}_2} \left[C_6H_7 \begin{matrix} -(NHCOØ)_2 \\ -(OH)_3 \end{matrix} \right]$$

4 moles HIO$_4$

2 moles HIO$_4$

[Dialdehyde]

Fig. 3.2. Kuehl et al. (K1).

$$\begin{matrix} \text{H} & \text{H} \\ \text{OCHCCH}_2\text{CCHO} \\ | & | \\ \text{ØCONH} & \text{NHCOØ} \end{matrix} \xrightarrow[\text{HCl}]{\text{EtSH}}$$

[Dialdehyde]

$$\begin{matrix} \text{EtS} & & & \text{SEt} \\ \backslash & \text{H} & \text{H} & / \\ & \text{CHCCH}_2\text{CCH} \\ / & | & | & \backslash \\ \text{EtS} & \text{ØCONH} & \text{NHCOØ} & \text{SEt} \end{matrix} \xrightarrow[\text{H}_2]{\text{Raney Ni}} \begin{matrix} \text{H} & \text{H} \\ \text{CH}_3\text{CCH}_2\text{CCH}_3 \\ | & | \\ \text{ØCONH} & \text{NHCOØ} \\ & meso \end{matrix}$$

(2) Separate
(1) ØCOCl

$$\text{CH}_3\text{COCH}_2\text{COCH}_3 \xrightarrow{\text{H}_2\text{NOH}} \begin{matrix} \text{CH}_3\text{CCH}_2\text{CCH}_3 \\ \| & \| \\ \text{HON} & \text{NOH} \end{matrix} \xrightarrow{[H]} \begin{matrix} \text{CH}_3\text{CHCH}_2\text{CHCH}_3 \\ | & | \\ \text{NH}_2 & \text{NH}_2 \end{matrix}$$

Fig. 3.3. Kuehl et al. (K1).

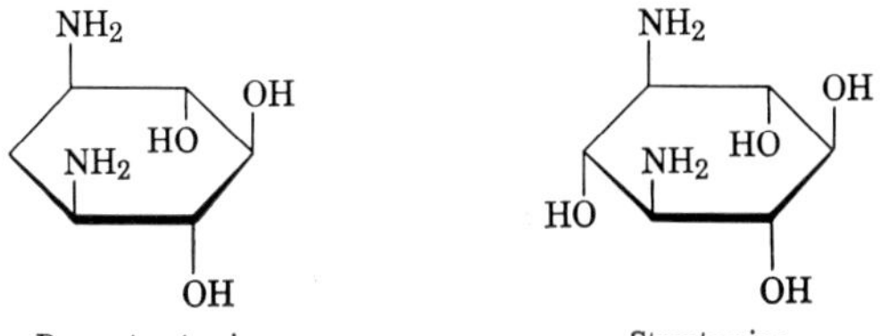

Deoxystreptamine   Streptamine

Fig. 3.4

tamine was shown to be a 1,3-diamino-4,5,6-trihydroxycyclo-hexane.

Stereochemistry of the compound was suggested by these workers (K1) to be all-*trans*, by analogy to the stereochem-istry of the earlier streptamine (see Fig. 3.4).

Streptamine

In this connection it is perhaps of value to examine the argument for the stereochemistry of streptamine itself. Streptamine is obtained by basic hydrolysis of its derivative, streptidine (Fig. 3.5), which in turn is obtained from acidic hydrolysis of streptomycin. The structure of streptamine was established by the combined efforts of groups at Merck and Company, the Squibb Institute for Medical Research, Ohio State University, and the University of Illinois. Streptamine consumes 6 moles of periodate to give 2 moles of ammonia but no formaldehyde; thus the hexa-substituted cyclohexane structure is established (C2, P4). The N,N'-diacetyl derivative of streptamine, on the other hand, con-sumes only 2 moles of periodate, indicating that the amino groups are 1,3- or 1,4- with respect to one another (C2, P4). A decision between these two alternative positions for the

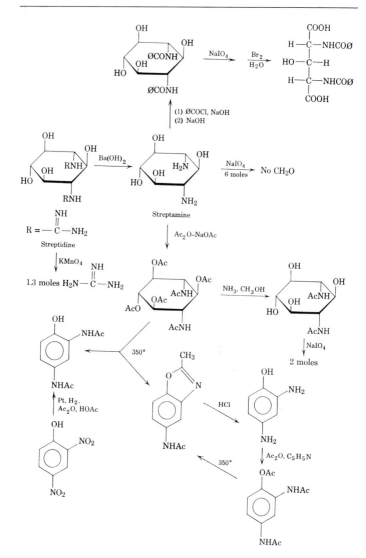

Fig. 3.5. Carter et al. (C2, C4), Peck et al. (P4).

amino groups was reached by the isolation of derivatives of a dibenzamidohydroxyglutaraldehyde (C4) and by the pyrolysis of hexaacetylstreptamine, which gave two benzene derivatives in which the nitrogens were 1,3- with respect to one another (Fig. 3.5). One of these was identical with the product of reductive acetylation of 2,4-dinitrophenol (P4). In these two ways streptamine was shown to be a 1,3-diamino-2,4,5,6-tetrahydroxycyclohexane.

Since streptamine is optically inactive, the two amino groups must be *cis* to one another. The 4- and 6-hydroxyl groups must be *cis* to one another as well. Additional stereochemistry of the molecule was established in the work of Wintersteiner and Klingsberg (W2) and synthetic experiments of Wolfrom and his coworkers (W3). The former workers N-acetylated, then O-methylated streptamine, removed the acetyl groups by acidic hydrolysis and, finally, oxidized the resulting tetra-O-methyldiamino compound to a D,L-mixture of dimethoxysuccinic acids (Fig. 3.6). This experiment establishes that the three vicinal hydroxyl groups are all-*trans* with respect to one another, since an all-*cis* linkage would have given *meso*-dimethoxysuccinic acid.

Streptamine was ultimately synthesized (Fig. 3.7) by the Ohio State group (W3). The stereochemistry of the starting material, D-glucosamine, established that the amino groups and the 5-hydroxyl group of streptamine must be *trans* to the 4- and 6-hydroxyl groups. D-Glucosamine was converted to its N-acetyl derivative, thence to the diethyl mercaptal, which on mercuric hydrolysis gave a 1-ethyl-mercaptofuranoside (Fig. 3.7). Lead tetraacetate cleavage of this compound gave an aldehyde, which was condensed with nitromethane to a mixture of 6-nitro derivatives. These were separated and the glucose mercaptide derivative was hydrolyzed, then subjected to basic condensation conditions to give the ring-closed nitrocyclohexane, which

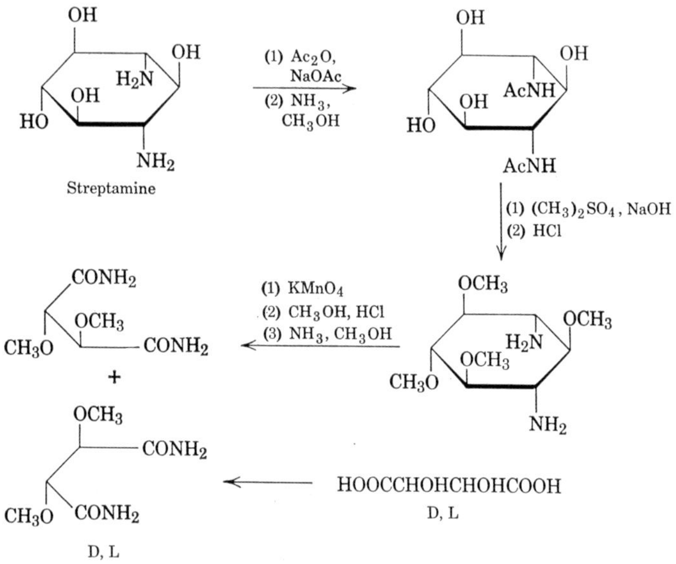

Fig. 3.6. Wintersteiner and Klingsberg (W2).

on reduction and separation of isomers gave streptamine. The assumption was made that under basic conditions the labile 3-nitro group and the 2- and 4-hydroxyl groups would all assume the more stable *trans* conformation.

In point of fact, both the 3-amino and the 4-hydroxyl groups had been established stereochemically by other means, so that only the C-2 hydroxyl was in question. Its configuration, *trans* to the adjacent amino groups, was established (and the remainder of the molecule's stereochemistry confirmed) by the subsequent conversion (with inversion at C-3) of streptamine to an inosamine (W5), whose stereochemistry was established (Fig. 3.8) by its synthesis from reduction of (±)-*epi*-inosose oxime (S6). The

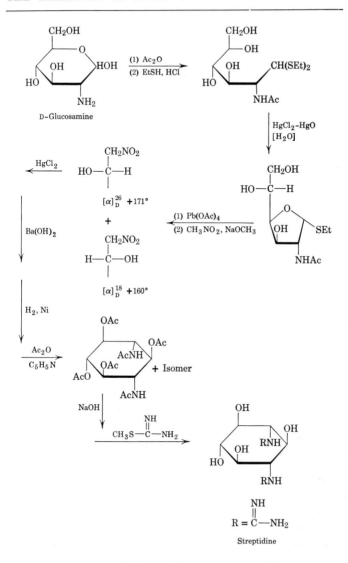

Fig. 3.7. Wolfrom, Olin, and Polglase (W3).

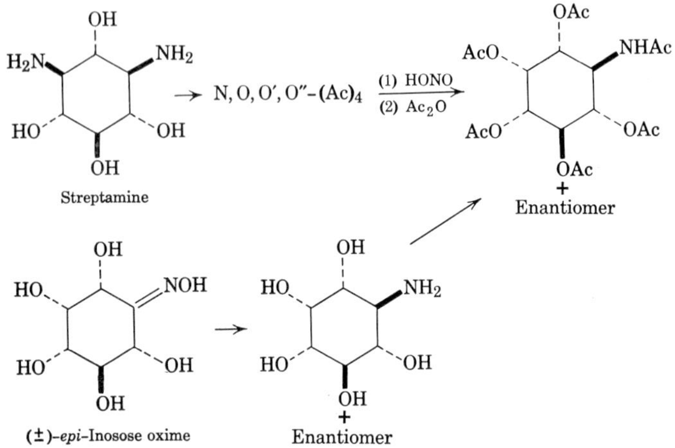

Fig. 3.8. Wintersteiner and Klingsberg (W5), Straube-Rieke et al. (S6).

n.m.r. spectrum of N-tetramethylstreptamine, recently interpreted by Slomp and MacKellar (S5), is in agreement with the accepted stereochemistry.

With streptamine's stereochemistry established, it is appropriate to return to deoxystreptamine.

Stereochemistry of Deoxystreptamine

Evidence other than analogy has been derived indicating the all-*trans* stereochemistry of this molecule. First, the amino groups must be *cis* to one another from the optical inactivity of the molecule, and the hydroxyl groups in the 4- and 6-positions must be *cis* to one another for the same reason. Next, the 3-amino group was shown to be *trans* to the 4-hydroxyl group, since N,N'-dibenzoyldeoxystreptamine did not undergo N→O benzoyl migration in mild

acid (D3), under conditions shown to effect such rearrangement for *cis*-2-hydroxybenzamidocyclohexane, but not for
the *trans* compound (Fig. 3.9). Carter and Dyer also assigned the 4,5,6-triol group an all-*trans* configuration, since
the rate of periodate uptake by N,N'-dibenzoyldeoxystrep-
tamine was nearly identical to that of N,N'-dibenzoylstrep-
tamine itself (D3), in which the 4,5,6-triol grouping had
definitely been established to be in the all-*trans* configuration.

Evidence for the all-*trans* stereochemistry of deoxystreptamine may also be derived from electrophoretic data (Table
3.2). The complete lack of migration of N,N'-diacetyl-
deoxystreptamine in borate electrophoresis is like that of
the all-*trans* *scyllo*-inositol, while inositols containing even
one *axial* hydroxyl (hence a *cis*-glycol grouping) migrate
much more rapidly.

Definitive evidence for the stereochemistry of deoxystreptamine recently has been obtained by Lemieux (L4) from

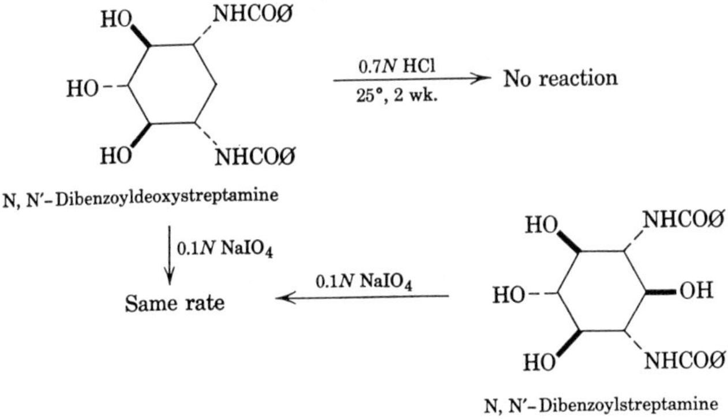

Fig. 3.9. Carter and Dyer (C3, D3).

TABLE 3.2

Electrophoresis Data

Compound	M_G	Ref.
N,N'-Diacetyldeoxy-streptamine	*ca.* 0.00 [a]	(H8)
scyllo-Inositol	[6*e*] 0.05	(A1, F2)
myo-	[1*a*, 5*e*] 0.53	(A1, F2)
(+)- or (−)-	[2*a*, 4*e*] 0.63	(A1, F2)
epi-	[2*a*, 4*e*] 0.73	(A1, F2)
allo-	[3*a*, 3*e*] 0.88	(A1, F2)
muco-	[3*a*, 3*e*] 0.96	(A1, F2)

[a] Migration relative to glucose, in 0.1*M* borate buffer.

the n.m.r. spectra of deoxystreptamine and the derivative shown in Fig. 3.10. The splitting pattern of the C-2 axial hydrogen of deoxystreptamine shows that all hydrogens on adjacent carbons must be axial; hence the substituent amino groups must be equatorial. The coupling constants of the protons at C-4 and C-6 of the derivative (Fig. 3.10) show that they must also be axial, split by two axial hydrogens on adjacent carbons. Thus all substituents in the

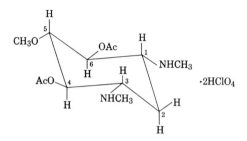

Fig. 3.10. Lemieux and Cushley (L4).

molecule must be equatorial and the all-*trans* stereochemistry is derived.

NEOSAMINE C AND NEAMINE

The second fragment of neamine earlier had been assumed to be a diaminohexose, since a reducing spot was obtained on a papergram of the vigorous acid hydrolyzate (D3). No structural assignments could be made, however, since, under the vigorous conditions required to effect cleavage of neamine, the diaminohexose decomposed and isolation was impossible. The diaminohexose ultimately was isolated by a modification of the method employed for the mild acid cleavage of neobiosamines B and C (C3). Neamine was converted to its tetra-N-acetyl derivative (Fig. 3.11), and this was hydrolyzed under relatively mild conditions. Chromatography of the hydrolyzate over a Dowex-

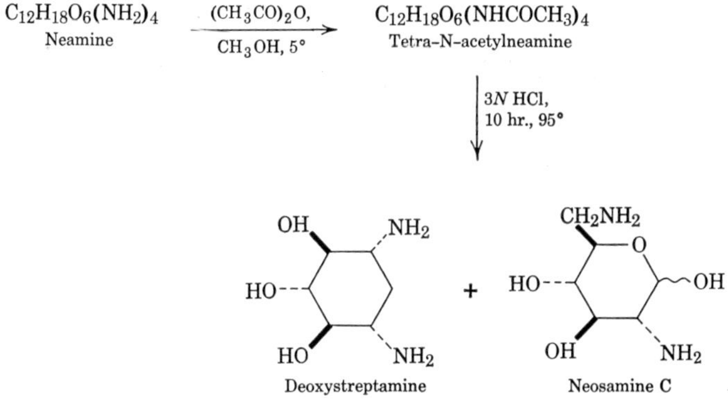

$$C_{12}H_{18}O_6(NH_2)_4 \xrightarrow[\text{CH}_3\text{OH, 5°}]{(CH_3CO)_2O,} C_{12}H_{18}O_6(NHCOCH_3)_4$$

Neamine   Tetra–N–acetylneamine

3*N* HCl,
10 hr., 95°

Deoxystreptamine   +   Neosamine C

Fig. 3.11. Hichens (C3).

50 ion exchange resin gave deoxystreptamine and the diaminohexose, which was identified by comparison of its properties and those of its N,N'-diacetyl derivative as neosamine C.

Periodate oxidation of tetra-N-acetylneamine showed conclusively that neosamine C exists in the pyranose form in neamine and that it is attached to the C-4 hydroxyl of deoxystreptamine. With only two hydroxyl groups in neosamine C and only two in deoxystreptamine in tetra-N-acetylneamine, the maximum periodate uptake would be 2 moles. This was, indeed, the amount taken up by the derivative (C3), establishing the structure shown in Fig. 3.12. The α-linkage of neosamine C was established by application of Hudson's rules of isorotation (C3). The contribution of the anomeric center from this calculation (Fig. 3.12) is seen to be +31,800, a value consistent only with an α-linkage. This, like the α-linkages of the neosamines in the neobiosamines, has been confirmed (R11) by n.m.r., in that the coupling constant of the H-1, H-2 protons of neosamine C of neamine in tetra-N-acetylneamine is 3.5 c.p.s., consistent only with *cis* H-1, H-2 stereochemistry.

The last remaining stereochemical point in neamine is

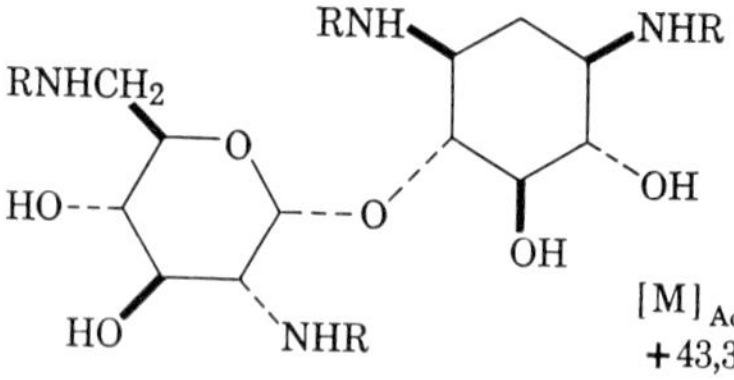

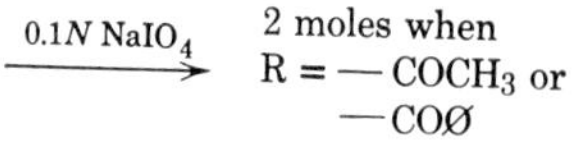

$$[M]_{AcNe} = [M]_{AcDe} + A_{AcC} + B_{AcC}$$
$$+43,300 = -3900 + A_{AcC} + 15,400$$
$$A_{AcC} = +31,800$$

Fig. 3.12.   Carter et al. (C3).

the asymmetry of deoxystreptamine in neamine—whether neosamine C is linked to deoxystreptamine at its 4- or 6-position. This problem has been solved (the correct formula is represented in Fig. 3.12) by means of cuprammonium complexes (H2) and is discussed in the next chapter.

4

THE INTACT NEOMYCINS
AND THE GLYCOSIDIC LINKAGES

POSITION OF NEOBIOSAMINE-NEAMINE LINKAGE

The position of attachment of neobiosamine B to neamine in neomycin B has been established by Schaffner and Schillings, and similar work by Carter and Georgiadis has located the position of attachment in neomycin C (R9). In each case the hexa-N-acetyl derivative of the appropriate neomycin was oxidized with periodate, then hydrolyzed. Deoxystreptamine was obtained in good yield from both N-acetylneomycins B and C (Fig. 4.1). In order to protect the deoxystreptamine moiety from periodate oxidation the neobiosamine must be attached to deoxystreptamine (rather than neosamine C). From the ease of hydrolysis of the glycosidic bond joining neobiosamine to neamine it could be assumed that the linkage is on the C-5 hydroxyl of deoxystreptamine, particularly since kanamycin, in which the glycosidic linkages are attached to C-4 and C-6, is resistant to hydrolysis. This point was firmly established by periodate oxidation of neomycins B and C (Fig. 4.1). Hydrolysis of the periodate product gave no deoxystreptamine, showing

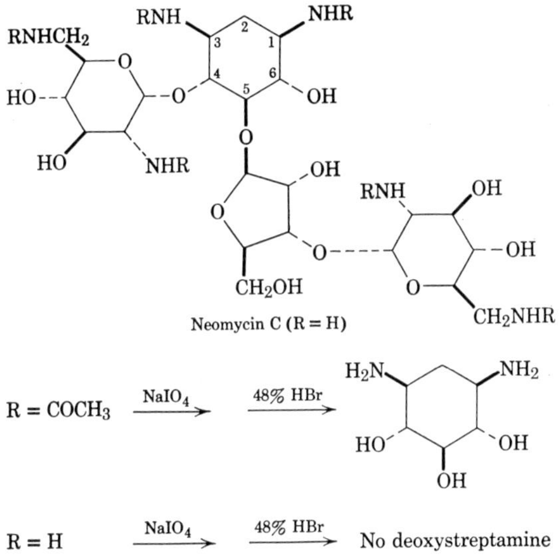

Fig. 4.1. Carter and Georgiadis, Schaffner and Schillings (R9).

that the linkage must have been on C-5 rather than on C-6, in order to allow periodate attack on the deoxystreptamine moiety.

RIBOSE IN NEOMYCINS B AND C

The structures of the neomycins are, then, established by evidence presented thus far, except for the nature of ribose in the intact neomycin and the question of the absolute stereochemistry of deoxystreptamine in neamine. In both antibiotics ribose recently has been shown, by methylation studies, to exist in the furanose form (R9). Hexa-N-acetyl-

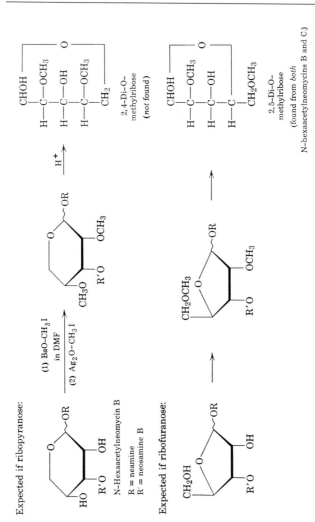

Fig. 4.2.   Hichens (R9).

neomycin B was treated with barium oxide and methyl iodide in dimethyl formamide (Fig. 4.2). This nearly completely O-methylated material was then hydrolyzed. Paper chromatography of the neutral products showed two compounds, whose R_F values are compared with those of known substances in Table 4.1. As seen from this table, a combination of electrophoretic and paper chromatographic data definitely assigns the structure of these riboses as 2-O-methylribose and 2,5-O,O'-dimethylribose. Both compounds could only arise from a 3-substituted ribose, and the latter only from ribose in the furanose form; the former must have come from partially methylated starting material. Authentic samples of the methylated riboses obtained from hydrolysis were prepared by an earlier route (Fig. 4.3).

Similar methylation and subsequent hydrolysis (R9) of hexa-N-acetylneomycin C gave the same two methylated riboses, 2-O-methyl- and 2,5-di-O-methylribose (Table 4.1), rather than the 3,4- or 3,5-di-O-methylriboses expected (Fig. 4.4). Ribose is thus seen to exist in the furanose form in

TABLE 4.1

Identity of Methylated Riboses

	O-Me Position						
	2-	3-	5-	2,5-	2,4-	2,3-	3,5-
R_F (BAW 415)							
Literature (B2)	0.46	0.49	0.49	0.69	0.61	0.64	0.69
Preparation (R9)	0.46		0.48	0.68	0.60		
O-Me-HAN-B (R9)	0.46			0.68			
-C (R9)	0.46			0.68			
M_{ribose} (borate)							
Literature (B2)	0.50	0.90	0.99	0.02		0.0	0.90
Preparation (R9)	0.49			0.0			
O-Me-HAN-B (R9)	0.51			0.0			
-C (R9)	0.50			0.0			

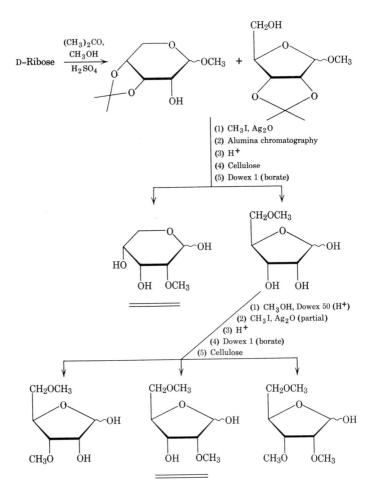

Fig. 4.3. Barker (B2), Hichens (R9).

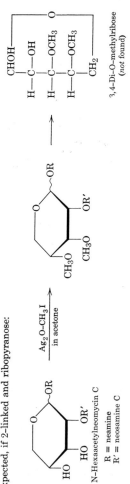

Expected, if 2-linked and ribopyranose:

N-Hexaacetylneomycin C

R = neamine
R′ = neosamine C

$\xrightarrow{\text{Ag}_2\text{O}-\text{CH}_3\text{I}}$ in acetone

CHOH—C—OH (H)—C—OCH$_3$ (H)—C—OCH$_3$ (H)—CH$_2$

3,4-Di-O-methylribose
(*not found*)

Expected, if 2-linked and ribofuranose:

CHOH—C—OH (H)—C—OCH$_3$ (H)—C—H—CH$_2$OCH$_3$

3,5-Di-O-methylribose
(*not found*)

Fig. 4.4. Hichens (R9).

neomycin C as well. The point of interest here, however, is the definitive assignment of attachment of neosamine C to the 3-position of ribose rather than the 2-, as deduced from periodate data. Methylation experiments are considered more reliable than periodate, which are subject to considerable interpretation; thus the earlier C-2 assignment is considered to have been in error.

It is exceedingly difficult to assign α or β stereochemistry to the glycosidic link between neobiosamine B (or C) and neamine in neomycin B (or C) by rotational considerations. Strict application of Hudson's rules is not possible since the required methyl α- and β-neobiosaminides are not available with ribose in the furanose form. Application of the rules employing the approximation used (R6) in the assignment of glycosidic linkage in neobiosamines B and C is possible, but somewhat unsatisfactory. The molecular rotation of neamine is $+39,600$, that of neobiosamine B is $+10,530$, and that of neomycin B is $+51,200$. Subtraction of the first two from the third gives a value of $+1100$ for the contribution of the anomeric center (Fig. 4.5). This value is neither strongly positive nor strongly negative and does not allow unequivocal α- or β-assignment. The same is true for calculations involving neobiosamine C, neamine, and neomycin C (Fig. 4.5).

It may be noted, however, that the mutarotation value of neobiosamine B is obtained with the disaccharide ribose largely in the pyranose form, whereas in neomycin B the ribose moiety is in the furanose form. Conversion of ribose derivatives from the pyranose to the furanose ring form invariably gives rise to an increased positive rotation. Allowance may be made for this by comparing the rotations of

Neobiosamine B + B + neamine = neomycin B
     + 10,530 + B + 39,600 = +51,200
                          B = +1100

Neobiosamine C + B + neamine = neomycin C
     + 32,200 + B + 39,600 = +74,600
                          B = +2800

                 D-Ribose + B = methyl β-ribofuranoside
                    − 3450 + B = − 10,200
                          B = − 6700

                 D-Ribose + B = methyl α-ribofuranoside
                    − 3450 + B = + 17,200
                          B = + 20,700

Fig. 4.5

methyl α-ribofuranoside, methyl β-ribofuranoside and ribose (mutarotation mixture, largely pyranose). The positive addendum in going from mutarotation ribose to methyl α-ribofuranoside is +20,700; the negative contribution in going to methyl β-ribofuranoside is −6700. The value obtained for neomycin B (+1100) lies between these two numbers, but it is considerably closer to that for the β-contribution (Fig. 4.5). Thus, with approximately 72% certainty one could assign a β-configuration to the ribofuranose portion of neomycin B (R11).

Similar arguments obtain for the anomeric contribution of +2800 in neomycin C. Even here, this value is closer to the mutarotation ribose→methyl β-ribofuranoside increment than to the corresponding α-increment (Fig. 4.5), although the probability is only about 65%. It is nearly certain that the stereochemistry of ribose is the same in both anomers, particularly since the glycosidic linkages of the other portions of the molecule are the same in both compounds; thus the probability of the β-linkage is enhanced.

This unsatisfactory assignment recently has been resolved by n.m.r. spectroscopy. Although the coupling constants of H-1, H-2 can vary over wide ranges in both α- and β-ribofuranosides, only in β-ribofuranosides (*trans* H-1, H-2) can they approach 0 (J1). Fortunately, this is the case in the coupling of the ribose anomeric proton, $J_{12} \cong 1$ c.p.s., in N-hexaacetylneomycins B and C, so that the β-glycosidic assignment is definitive.

ABSOLUTE STEREOCHEMISTRY OF DEOXYSTREPTAMINE

From the total evidence presented thus far, then, the structures of neomycins B and C are assigned, except for one point of stereochemistry not yet dealt with, that of deoxystreptamine in neamine. Although deoxystreptamine itself is optically inactive, the introduction of a substituent in the C-4 or C-6 position (or C-1 or C-3) gives rise to an

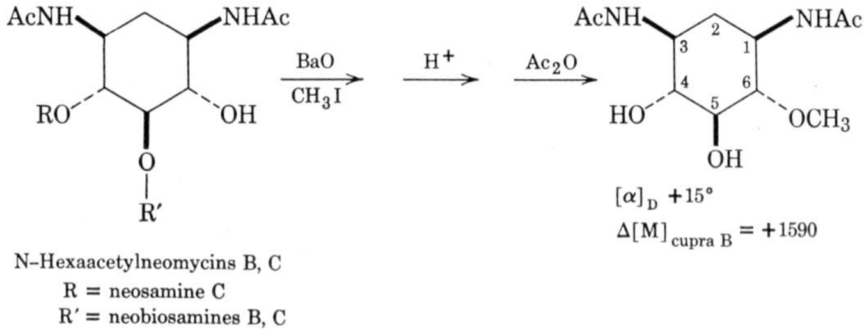

N–Hexaacetylneomycins B, C
   R = neosamine C
   R′ = neobiosamines B, C

Fig. 4.6.   Hichens (H2).

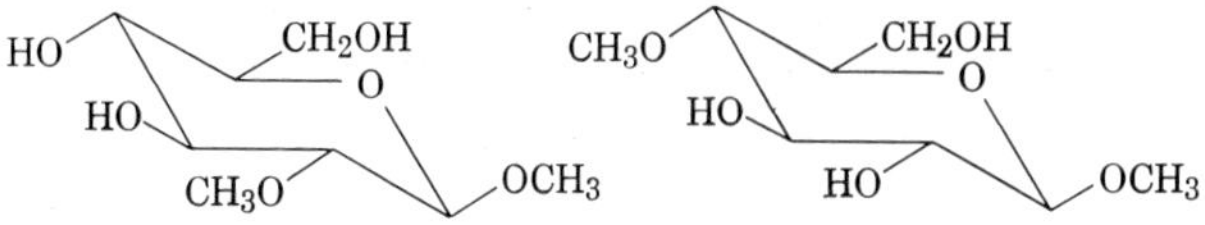

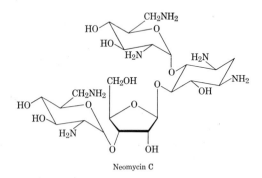

$\Delta[M]_{\text{cupra B}} = +2190$ $\Delta[M]_{\text{cupra B}} = -2020$

$\Delta[M]_{436} = [M]_{436} \text{ (cuprammonium)} - [M]_{436} \text{ (H}_2\text{O)}$

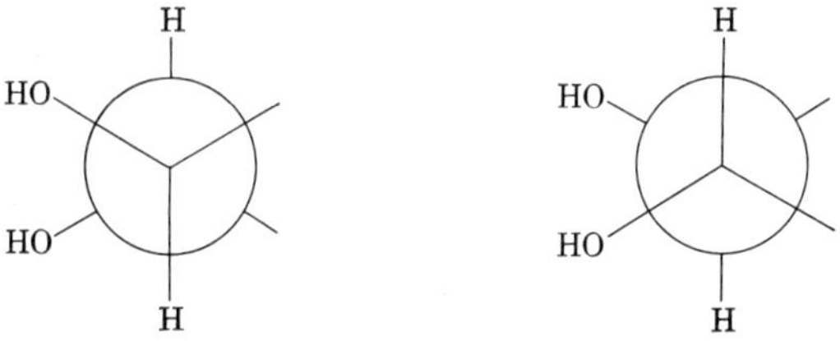

A   B

Fig. 4.7. Reeves (R13).

Neomycin C

Fig. 4.8.

asymmetric molecule. This may be seen by the rotation of di-N-acetyl-6-O-methyldeoxystreptamine ($[\alpha]_D + 15°$) isolated from O-methylation of N-acetylneomycin B and subsequent hydrolysis and reacetylation [Fig. 4.6 (R9)]. The absolute stereochemistry of this molecule has been assigned recently (H2) from its strongly positive rotation in cuprammonium solution, characteristic of pyranose vicinal glycols (R13) of the relative configuration A (Fig. 4.7). Vicinal glycols of the relative configuration B (Fig. 4.7) give strongly negative shifts in cuprammonium solution. Since the absolute configuration of the mono-O-methyldeoxystreptamine is thus established as that in Fig. 4.6, the neosamine must have occupied the hydroxyl shown (at C-4) in deoxystreptamine.

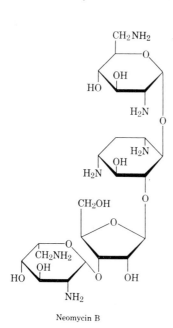

Neomycin B

Fig. 4.9

In conclusion, then, the structure of neomycin C has been established firmly to be that shown in Figs. 4.1 and 4.8 (conformational). The structure of neomycin B is also settled except for the configurations at the central carbon atoms of the neosamine B fragment, where further study is required. The presently most probable structure for neomycin B is presented in Fig. 4.9.

ADDENDUM

Since the structure of neosamine B has now been established firmly (C12, R17, H19, R18), the structure given for neomycin B (Fig. 4.9) is also certain.

The stereochemistry of deoxystreptamine in neamine and paromamine (see Chapter 5) has now been established chemically by Tatsuoka and Horii (T3); the results are in agreement with those from the previously reported cuprammonium procedure (H2, R20, R21). The chemical route, outlined in Fig. 4.10, proceeds from the unsymmetrical di-O-methyldeoxystreptamine described earlier (H2, T4). Isolation in small yield of di-O-methyl-D-(+)-tartaric acid establishes the stereochemistry of the unsymmetrical deoxystreptamine diol in neamine and paromamine to be as shown.

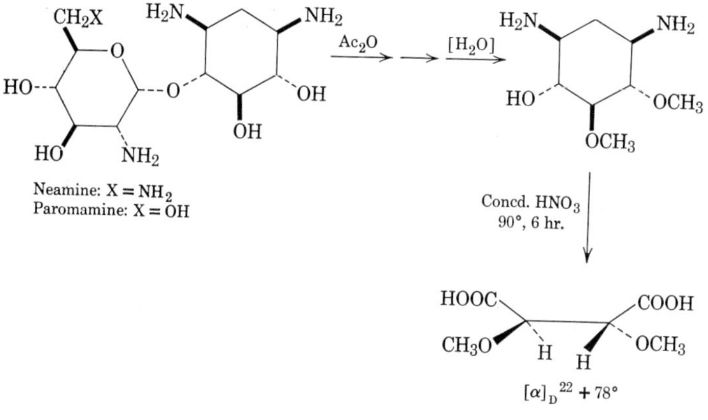

Fig. 4.10. Tatsuoka and Horii (T3).

5

RELATED ANTIBIOTICS

In the preceding chapter the structure of neomycin B was deduced to be that of Fig. 4.9 and that of neomycin C (Fig. 4.8) was shown to differ only in a single asymmetric center—the C-5 position of the neosamine moiety of neo-biosamine. During the last ten years a number of anti-biotics closely and distantly related to the neomycins have been discovered, and the structures of many of these have been elucidated. This chapter attempts to correlate the structures of these related antibiotics.

OTHER NEOMYCINS AND OTHER ANTIBIOTICS FROM *S. fradiae*

As has been noted from the outset, the usual neomycin complex consists of two distinct antibiotics, neomycins B and C, whose structures have recently been established. The former neomycin A is now known to be a degradation product of both of these—neamine. More recently, two new neomycins have been isolated from cultures of *Strepto-myces fradiae*. At present, these are referred to only as neomycins LP-I and LP-II, in which the term LP refers to the observed low potency of these materials. The presence of material other than neomycins B and C was suspected in a culture which produced neomycin of lower than usual activity, and recent work by Chilton (C1) has demonstrated that there are, in fact, two LP neomycins in the antibiotic obtained from this strain. The mixture of neomycins B and C, LP-I and LP-II has been separated effectively on charcoal, employing the procedure of Ford et al. (F1), but with a higher ratio of charcoal to substrate. Preliminary investigations of neomycins LP-I and LP-II have shown them to be interesting compounds. On methanolysis and chromatography over an ion exchange resin each gives two large fragments—methyl neobiosaminide and neamine, very small peaks—ribose and neosamine, and a fifth, large peak which is an N-acetyl derivative of neamine. That neomycins LP-I and LP-II are mono-N-acetyl derivatives of neomycins B and C (with N-acetylation in the neamine fragment) seems very likely.

In addition to neomycins B and C, LP-I and LP-II, other materials of antibiotic activity have been isolated at various times from *Streptomyces fradiae*. These include an antibiotic completely unrelated to neomycin, called fradicin (S10), whose molecular formula has been suggested to be $C_{30}H_{34}N_4O_4$ (Table 5.1), and other less well-defined materials whose existence has not been thoroughly substantiated (L6).

A number of other antibiotics have been reported at one time or another which have subsequently been shown to be identical with neomycin B or C (Table 5.2). Thus, streptothricin BI was shown to be identical to neomycin C and streptothricin BII to neomycin B (M2). Similarly, the antibiotics dextromycin (T2) and flavomycin (A4) have

TABLE 5.1

Other Antibiotics from S. fradiae

Neomycins LP-I and LP-II
  N-Acetyl derivatives of neomycins B and C

Fradicin
  Antifungal
  $C_{30}H_{34}N_4O_4$ (?)
  Sol. $CHCl_3$, sl. sol. H_2O

been reported to be identical to neomycin, and others, notably fradiomycin and colimycin [a Russian antibiotic unrelated to the Italian-Japanese antibiotic ($=$colistin) of the same name], are assumed to be identical (M6, S7). This list does not even include formulary or trade names for the neomycins.

Recently the antibiotic framycetin (soframycin) was shown to be identical to neomycin B with a small amount of added neomycin C. Due to the great water solubility of the neomycins and their degradation products and the very closely related structures of many of the degradation products, it is exceedingly difficult to establish the identity

TABLE 5.2

Antibiotics Identical to the Neomycins

Streptothricin BI (neomycin C)
Streptothricin BII (neomycin B)
Dextromycin (B, with a little C)
Framycetin (B, with a little C)
Flavomycin
Colimycin
Fradiomycin
Mycifradin

of antibiotics in this series. It may perhaps be worthwhile to review the steps which were necessary to establish the identity of neomycin B and framycetin (R1). The intact antibiotics had identical analyses and rotations and traveled together on paper chromatography (Table 5.3). More significantly, identity of rotation and chromatographic behavior was also shown for the N-acetyl derivatives of the two antibiotics. On mild methanolysis both antibiotics gave neamine, together with a second material, which was shown to be identical to methyl neobiosaminide B by paper chromatography, rotation, and further degradation to neosamine B and ribose. Since all the fragments of the two antibiotics are identical, the rotations of neobiosamine B and neomycin B establish the identity of linkages and the identity of the antibiotics. The last remaining possibility for isomerism was removed by the demonstration of identical periodate uptake data in the intact and N-acetylated antibiotics.

Definitions differ over what is required for a molecule to be a neomycin, but in a strict sense it must have a structure identical to that of neomycin B or C except for points of stereochemistry; i.e., a neomycin should contain neamine,

TABLE 5.3

Proof of Identity of Neomycin B and Framycetin

(1) Rotation
(2) Formula
(3) Paper chromatography of N-acetyl derivatives
(4) Methanolysis to neamine and methyl neobiosaminide B
(5) Hydrolysis of methyl neobiosaminide B to D-ribose
(6) Hydrolysis of MNB-B to neosamine B

TABLE 5.4

Deoxystreptamine Antibiotics

	Discovery of Group	Gross Structure
Neomycins B, C	Waksman and Leche-valier, 1949 (W1)	Rinehart, Carter, Schaffner, et al., 1962 (R9, H2)
Paromomycins I, II	Frohardt, Haskell, Ehrlich, and Knudsen, 1956 (F3)	Haskell, French, and Bartz, 1959 (H4, H2)
Kanamycins A, B, C	Umezawa et al., 1957 (T1)	Cron, Hooper, Lemieux, et al., 1958 (C5, H2)

a diaminohexose, and ribose. Thus far no compounds other than those already mentioned fit this description. On the other hand, there are a number of antibiotics closely related to the neomycins which, although they do not contain neamine, contain deoxystreptamine. A list of the deoxystreptamine antibiotics is shown in Table 5.4 and contains, in addition to the neomycins, the paromomycins and kanamycins.

PAROMOMYCINS

Of these, the paromomycins are most closely related to the neomycins. The structure of paromomycin I, as established in 1959 by Haskell, French and Bartz, is shown in Fig. 5.1; it differs from neomycin B in the replacement of the 6-amino group of neosamine C in neamine by a 6-hydroxyl group; i.e., paromamine is a glucosaminido-deoxystreptamine, whereas neamine is a neosaminido-deoxystreptamine. The proof of structure of paromomycin I follows rather closely that of the neomycins and is outlined in Figs. 5.1 to 5.5. Thus, methanolysis of paromomycin

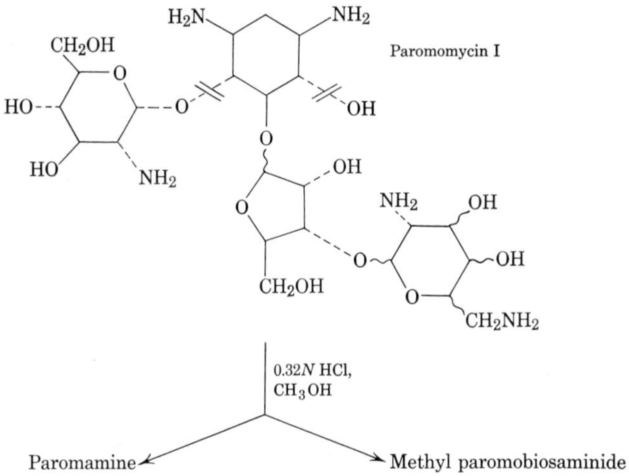

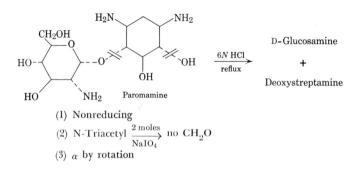

Fig. 5.1. Haskell, French, and Bartz (H5).

(H5) gives paromamine and methyl paromobiosaminide (Fig. 5.1).

The structure of paromamine (a nonreducing fragment) was established (H5) as shown in Fig. 5.2, where it may be seen that on vigorous hydrolysis deoxystreptamine and

(1) Nonreducing

(2) N-Triacetyl $\xrightarrow[\text{NaIO}_4]{\text{2 moles}}$ no CH_2O

(3) α by rotation

Fig. 5.2. Haskell, French, and Bartz (H5).

D-glucosamine are obtained. Tri-N-acetylparomamine consumed 2 moles of periodate, but gave no formaldehyde, thus
establishing the linkage at C-4 in deoxystreptamine and the
pyranose form of glucosamine in paromamine. An α-linkage of glucosamine in paromamine was established by rotational considerations. The absolute configuration of deoxystreptamine in paromamine was not assigned.

   The structure proof of paromobiosamine (H6) is outlined
in Fig. 5.3, where it is seen that hydrolysis of the N,N′-di-
benzoyl compound gave ribose, while vigorous hydrolysis
(6N hydrochloric acid) of the basic disaccharide gave
paromose. The gross structure of paromose follows from

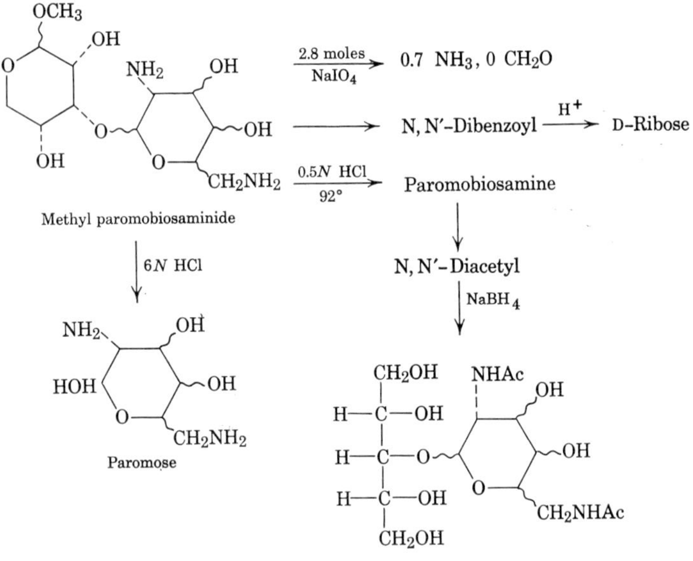

Fig. 5.3. Haskell, French, and Bartz (H6).

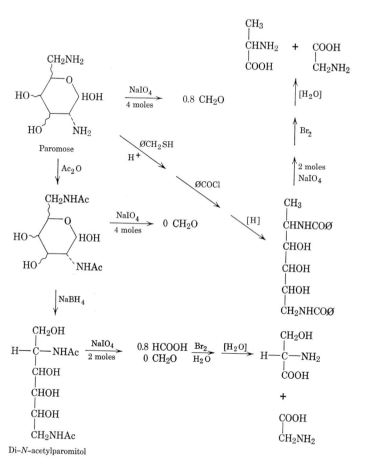

Fig. 5.4. Haskell, French, and Bartz (H6).

degradation data outlined in Fig. 5.4. In particular, di-N-acetylparomitol on periodate oxidation, bromine water treatment, and hydrolysis gave L-serine, together with glycine, but no formaldehyde. This established a 2,6-diaminohexose and the C-2 configuration. Paromose could be converted to its benzyl mercaptal and the latter's N-benzoyl derivative, which, in turn, was reduced to the corresponding methyl compound. Oxidation of this and identification of alanine established the aldohexose possibility rather than the keto-hexose.

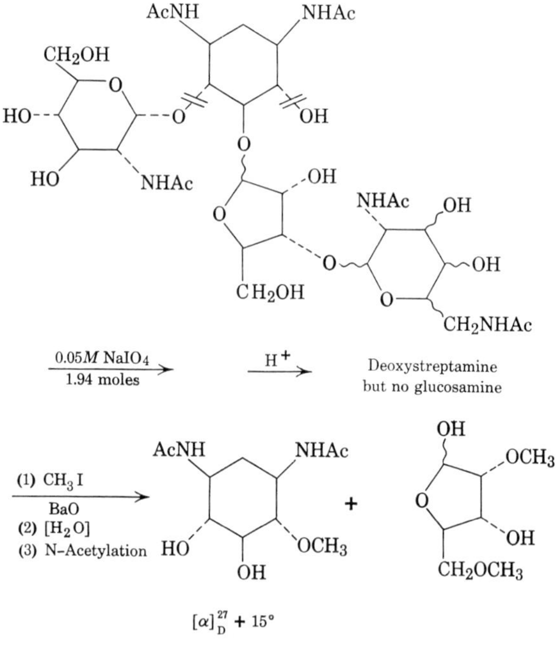

Fig. 5.5. Haskell, French, and Bartz (H4).

Periodate oxidation of methyl paromobiosaminide (Fig. 5.3) produced no formaldehyde, thus established the pyranose form for paromose in paromobiosamine. The linkage of paromose to ribose must be at the ribose C-3 position (H4) since methylation of penta-N-acetylparomomycin and subsequent hydrolysis gave 2,5-di-O-methylribose (Fig. 5.5), identified by comparison to authentic material. The C-5 link of paromobiosamine to paromamine is established by failure of periodate to attack the deoxystreptamine portion

TABLE 5.5

Properties of Neosamine B and Paromose Derivatives

	$[\alpha]_D$	Picrate Melting Point	Picrate $[\alpha]_D$	Ref.
Paromose	+19°	126–128°d.	+22°	(H6)
Neosamine B	+17.5°	125.0–126.5	+13°	(R1)
"Diaminohexose I"	+24° [a]	126–127° [a]	+9.4° [a]	(H9)
Paromobiosamine	+32°	—	—	(H6)
Neobiosamine	+34°	—	—	(R1)

	$[\alpha]_D$	R_{NAG} [b]	p-Nitrophenylhydrazone Melting Point	p-Nitrophenylhydrazone $[\alpha]_D$	Ref.
N,N'-Diacetyl-paromose	+5°		229–231°	+59° [c]	(H6)
			118–120°	+56° [d]	(H8)
N,N'-Diacetyl-neosamine B	+6°	1.8	215–218°d.	+160°	(H9)
	+5°		118–120°	+62° [d]	(H8)
"N,N'-Diacetyl-diaminohexose I"	+5°	1.8	215–218°d.	+162°	(H9)

	$[\alpha]_D$	Melting Point	Ref.
N,N'-Diacetyl-paromitol	−17.8°	150–151.5°	(H6)
	−24.5°	148–150°	(H8)
N,N'-Diacetyl-neosaminol B	−21°	147–149°	(H8)

[a] Slight "diaminohexose II" impurity.
[b] R_F relative to N-acetylglucosamine.
[c] Reported as 5.9° due to decimal point error.
[d] Undergoes slow mutarotation.

of N-acetylparomomycin and by the isolation of 6-O-methyl-deoxystreptamine from methylated N-acetylparomomycin.

Points of structure still remaining in paromomycin at the conclusion of the Parke-Davis group's earlier studies were the stereochemistry (except at C-2) of paromose, that of ribose at the C-1 position, and the absolute stereochemistry of the deoxystreptamine portion of the molecule. The first point was settled by establishing that paromose and paromobiosamine are identical with neosamine B and neobiosamine B, respectively. The properties of the free sugars were very suggestive of identity (Table 5.5), but the compounds appeared to be distinguished by the published rotations of their N-acetyl p-nitrophenylhydrazones (Table 5.5).

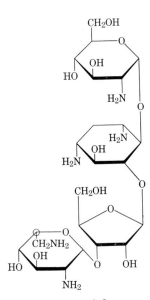

Paromomycin I

Paromomycin II is epimeric at the circled carbon atom.

Fig. 5.6

Part of the confusion was resolved when it was revealed that the earlier published rotation of N,N'-diacetylparomose p-nitrophenylhydrazone was in error by a factor of 10 (H7), and the revised rotation was in agreement with that obtained by Hichens (H8). These still did not agree, however, with the values obtained by Horii (H9) for his "diaminohexose I" from zygomycin A, which he showed to be identical with neosamine B (Table 5.5). Ultimate identity of neosamine B with paromose was established by a mixture melting point of the N,N'-diacetyl derivatives of paromitol and neosaminol B (R9).

The stereochemistry of ribose at C-1 and of neosamine B at C-1 in paromomycin I was established from the n.m.r. spectrum of N-pentaacetylparomomycin I by the same arguments employed for the ribose and neosamine linkages of the neomycins (R11). Moreover, since the same mono-O-methyldeoxystreptamine had been obtained from paromomycin I and neomycin B the absolute stereochemistry of deoxystreptamine in the two antibiotics is the same. Thus, the complete structure for paromomycin I may be written as in Fig. 5.6 (H2).

An isomer, paromomycin II, has also been isolated (R9). This compound contains D-glucosamine, deoxystreptamine, and D-ribose, but neosamine C instead of neosamine B. Thus its structure is most reasonably written as in Fig. 5.6.

Antibiotics Identical to the Paromomycins

Very recently, Schaffner and Schillings (S8) have shown in carefully controlled experiments that paromomycin is, in fact, identical with an earlier antibiotic, catenulin, and also with the more recent antibiotics hydroxymycin and amminosidin (Table 5.6). Identity of another antibiotic, monomycin (B3), must be suspected. Identity of these compounds was established by rotation, microanalyses, and paper chromatographic behavior of the antibiotics' N-acetyl derivatives, and also by chromatography of the products of hydrolysis of the N-acetyl derivatives. Here again, proof of identity was difficult, but it has been effected.

The antibiotic zygomycin A (H11) has also been shown to be identical to paromomycin. The zygomycins may be

TABLE 5.6

Antibiotics Identical with Paromomycin (S8)

Catenulin	(D5)
Hydroxymycin	(H10)
Amminosidin	(A5)
Zygomycin A	(H11)
Monomycin (?)	(B3)

separated chromatographically into zygomycins A and B (H13) (Fig. 5.7). Of these, zygomycin B resembles streptomycin in giving a positive Sakaguchi test but negative ninhydrin test, while zygomycin A is more closely related to neomycin and paromomycin in giving negative Sakaguchi but positive ninhydrin tests.

Zygomycin A was degraded in a fashion precisely analogous to that employed for the neomycins and for paromomycin (H9). Methanolysis, as is outlined in Fig. 5.8, gave pseudo-neamine (paromamine) and methyl zygobiosaminide. The latter compound was further hydrolyzed to ribose and to a mixture of diaminohexoses which were separated chromatographically as their N-acetyl derivatives. Thus, zygomycin A is a mixture of two antibiotics, just as paromomycin consists of paromomycins I and II and neomycin of

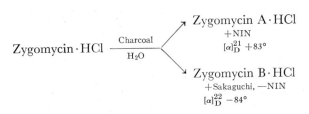

Fig. 5.7. Hitomi et al. (H13).

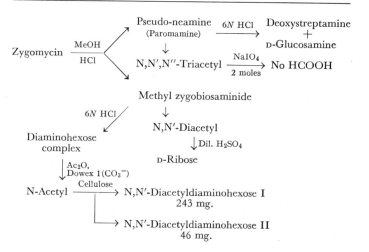

Fig. 5.8. Horii (H9).

neomycins B and C. The diaminohexose II was shown
(Table 2.3) to be identical to neosamine C (R10), while
the diaminohexose I was shown to be identical to neosamine B (H9) (Table 5.5). More recent studies (H20) have
confirmed the identity in every respect of zygomycin AI
with paromomycin I and of zygomycin AII with paromomycin II. Thus, the structures of the zygomycins A are also
those of Fig. 5.6.

KANAMYCINS

Somewhat further removed from the neomycin and paromomycin antibiotics are the kanamycins. These compounds
contain a central deoxystreptamine nucleus but no ribose.

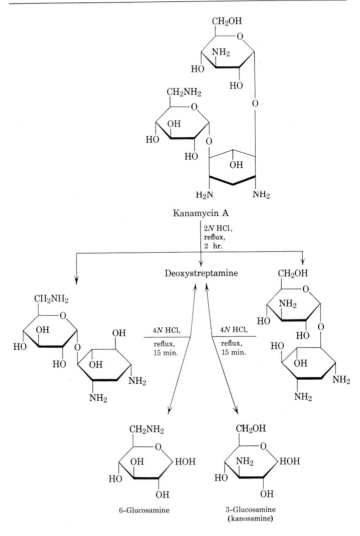

Fig. 5.9. Cron, Hooper, Lemieux, et al. (C6).

Linkage on the deoxystreptamine moiety is at the 4- and 6-positions, and in the major component, kanamycin A, the hexoses attached are 3-amino-3-deoxy-D-glucose and 6-amino-6-deoxy-D-glucose.

The structure of kanamycin A was demonstrated independently by two groups of workers, one working at Bristol Laboratories and the University of Ottawa (C5), the other in Japan (M3). The structural studies of the American-Canadian group will be discussed first. Rather mild hydrolysis of kanamycin A gave two fragments; each contained deoxystreptamine, but one contained, in addition, 3-aminoglucose and the other 6-aminoglucose (C6) (Fig. 5.9). Thus the central position of the deoxystreptamine moiety is established.

The proof of structure (C6) of 3-glucosamine (kanosamine) is outlined in Fig. 5.10. This includes periodate oxidation of N-acetylkanosamine, which consumed 1 mole of periodate and gave 1 mole of formic acid; the former observation eliminated a 4-, 5-, or 6-aminohexose and the latter a 2-aminohexose. Nitrous acid deamination of tetra-O-acetyl-kanosamine and reacetylation gave pentaacetylglucose. Ultimately, synthesis (C5) by the method of Peat and Wiggins (P6) gave an authentic sample of the material.

Similarly, the structure of 6-aminoglucose was established (C7) by the demonstration that the amino sugar and its N-acetyl derivative consumed identical quantities of periodate and by nitrous acid deamination of tetra-O-acetyl-6-aminoglucose and reacetylation to glucose pentaacetate (Fig. 5.11). This compound, as well, has been compared to synthetic material (C7, O4).

Periodate oxidation of kanamycin A destroyed both 3-glucosamine and 6-glucosamine but not deoxystreptamine (C5),

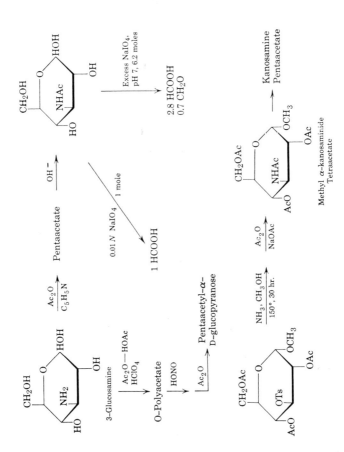

Fig. 5.10. Cron, Hooper, Lemieux, et al. (C6).

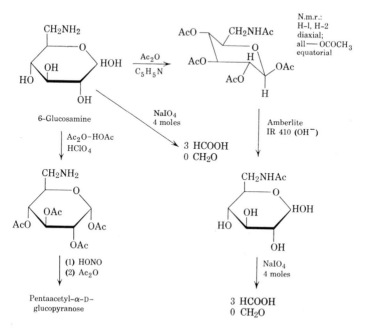

Fig. 5.11. Cron, Hooper, Lemieux, et al. (C7).

which established a 4- and 6-linkage in the molecule (Fig. 5.12). Periodate oxidation of the tetra-N-acetyl derivative consumed 2 moles of periodate and gave 1 mole of formic acid. Subsequent hydrolysis of the product gave deoxystreptamine and 3-glucosamine, but not 6-glucosamine. This oxidation established a pyranose form in both 3-glucosamine and 6-glucosamine. The α-linkage of both aminohexoses in kanamycin was established by the high positive contribution of the anomeric centers of each aminohexose in the poly-

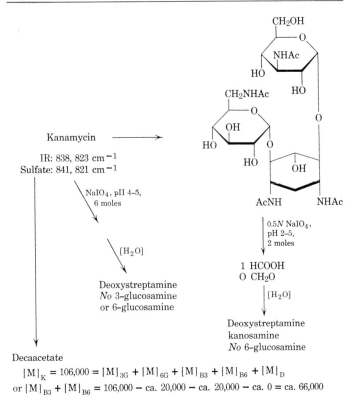

Kanamycin ⟶

IR: 838, 823 cm^{-1}
Sulfate: 841, 821 cm^{-1}

NaIO$_4$, pH 4–5,
6 moles

[H$_2$O]

Deoxystreptamine
No 3–glucosamine
or 6–glucosamine

0.5N NaIO$_4$,
pH 2–5,
2 moles

1 HCOOH
0 CH$_2$O

[H$_2$O]

Deoxystreptamine
kanosamine
No 6–glucosamine

Decaacetate

$[M]_K = 106,000 = [M]_{3G} + [M]_{6G} + [M]_{B3} + [M]_{B6} + [M]_D$

or $[M]_{B3} + [M]_{B6} = 106,000 - $ ca. $20,000 - $ ca. $20,000 - $ ca. $0 = $ ca. $66,000$

Fig. 5.12. Cron, Hooper, Lemieux, et al. (C5).

acetate, as well as by infrared bands attributable to the
α-linkages (C5).

The Japanese proof of structure of kanamycin A followed
a similar pattern. Methanolysis of kanamycin A gave the
known deoxystreptamine, plus methyl α-6-glucosaminide,
and methyl α-kanosaminide (O1). The structure (except

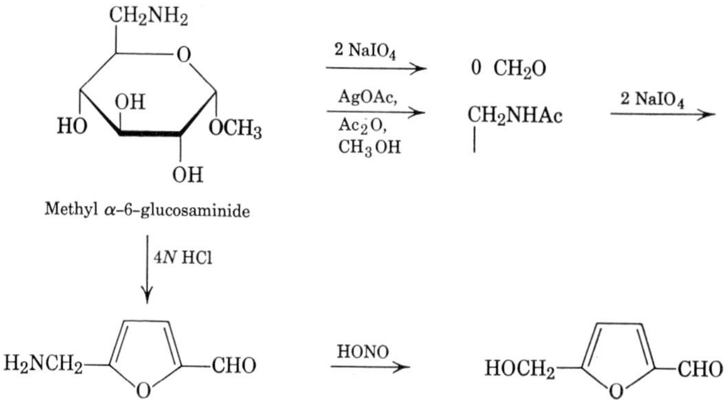

Fig. 5.13. Ogawa, Ito, Inoue, and Kondo (O2).

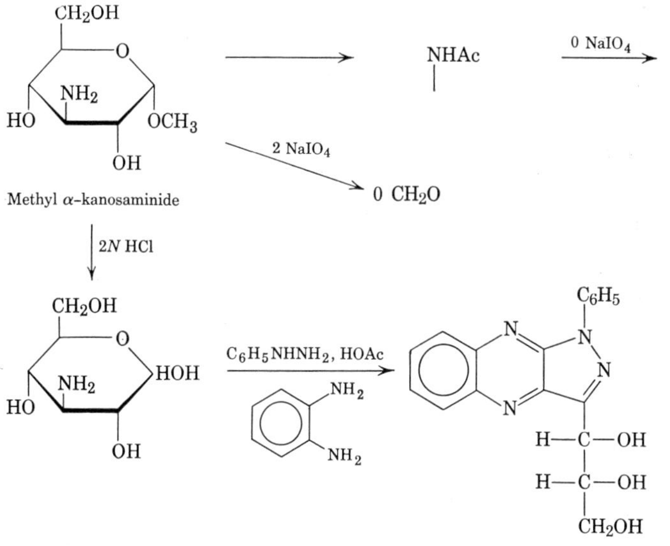

Fig. 5.14. Ogawa Ito, Inoue, and Kondo (O3).

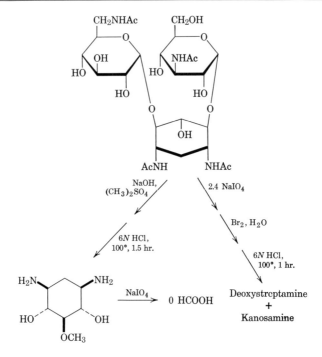

Fig. 5.15. Maeda, Murase, Umezawa, et al. (M5, U1).

stereochemistry) of methyl α-6-glucosaminide was established
(O2) by the 2-mole periodate uptake (without formaldehyde
formation) of the glycoside and its N-acetyl derivative and
its degradative hydrolysis to 5-aminomethylfurfural (Fig.
5.13).

The structure of methyl α-kanosaminide was then de-
termined (O3) by its 2-mole periodate uptake and by the
failure of its N-acetyl derivative to consume periodate. The
stereochemistry at C-4 and C-5 was established by its con-

version to 3-(D-erythro-1,2,3-trihydroxypropyl)-1-phenylfla-vazole (Fig. 5.14).

The structure of the intact antibiotic was then de-termined (Fig. 5.15) by the isolation of 5-O-methyldeoxy-streptamine (U1) and the demonstration of 2-mole periodate uptake by N-tetraacetylkanamycin A (M5).

Two additional kanamycins have been reported. Of these, kanamycin C (Fig. 5.16) resembles kanamycin A more in that its hydrolysis (M7) produces deoxystreptamine, kanosamine, and a monoaminohexose; the latter has been shown to be D-glucosamine. Moreover, the product of partial hydrolysis has been identified with paromamine (W11), which allows the assignment of absolute stereo-chemistry to the substituted deoxystreptamine (H2). The biogenetic similarity of kanamycins A and C also suggests the absolute stereochemistry of the former (shown in Figs. 5.9 and 5.12), as well as of kanamycin B (Fig. 5.17), which

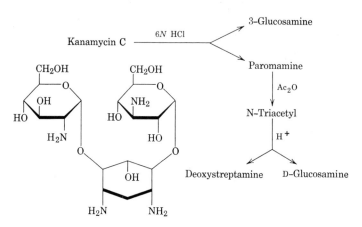

Fig. 5.16. Murase (M7), Wakazawa and Fukatsu (W11).

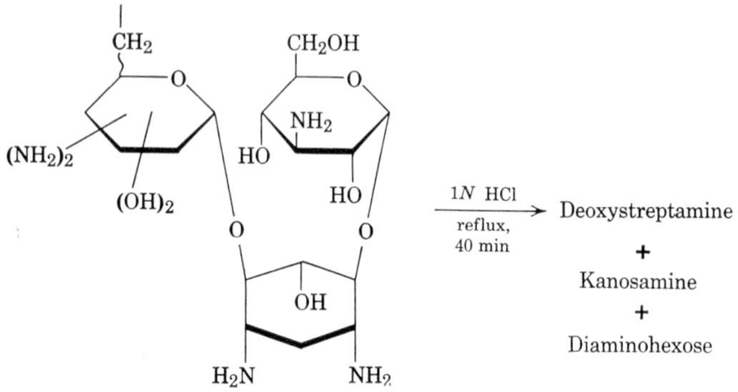

Kanamycin B

Fig. 5.17.   Schmitz, Hooper, et al. (S11).

has been shown to contain kanosamine, deoxystreptamine, and a diaminohexose (S11).   Nothing is reported about the structure of the diaminohexose, but it has been stated to be different from either neosamine B or neosamine C (H12). Biogenetic speculation would have suggested it to be ne- osamine C.

STREPTOMYCINS

To date no other antibiotics have been reported which contain the deoxystreptamine nucleus, although the very closely related streptamine molecule is, of course, found in streptomycin, as we have noted in Chapter 3.   The complete structure of streptomycin with certain stereochemistry per- haps in doubt is given in Fig. 5.18.   In streptomycin the

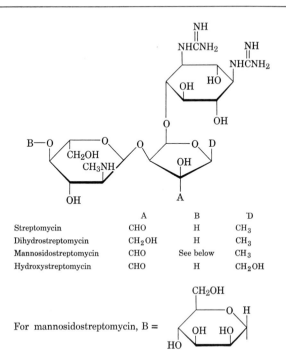

	A	B	D
Streptomycin	CHO	H	CH_3
Dihydrostreptomycin	CH_2OH	H	CH_3
Mannosidostreptomycin	CHO	See below	CH_3
Hydroxystreptomycin	CHO	H	CH_2OH

For mannosidostreptomycin, B =

Fig. 5.18

streptamine portion of the molecule is found with the amino groups in the form of their guanido derivatives. An amino sugar, N-methyl-L-glucosamine, also forms a portion of the streptomycin molecule. The chemistry of the streptomycins has been reviewed elsewhere (L7, V1, W6, W7). Another antibiotic shown to contain guanido groups, zygomycin B, has been noted as a second component of the zygomycins (H13), where zygomycin A is paromomycin.

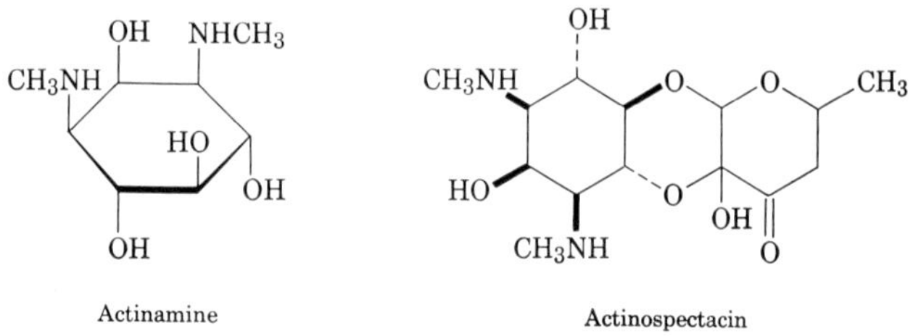

Actinamine

Actinospectacin

Fig. 5.19. Hoeksema, Argoudelis, and Wiley (H3).

ACTINOSPECTACIN

Another related antibiotic is actinospectacin, whose structure has been assigned only in the last few months. In this molecule is found the N,N'-dimethyl derivative of an inositol diamine which is stereoisomeric with streptamine. It has been named actinamine (W8), and its position of stereoisomerism is the C-2 hydroxyl group, which in actinamine has been shown to be axial by n.m.r. evidence, hence *cis* to the amino groups (S5). The same stereochemistry also has been assigned with the help of spin-spin decoupling techniques (C9). The novel complete structure assigned to actinospectacin (H3) is shown in Fig. 5.19. Other authors have presented related arguments (C10) for structures of degradation fragments.

INOSAMINE ANTIBIOTICS

Considerably less closely related is the antibiotic hygromycin, which contains the monoaminoinositol derivative *neo*-inosamine. This compound is present in both hygro-

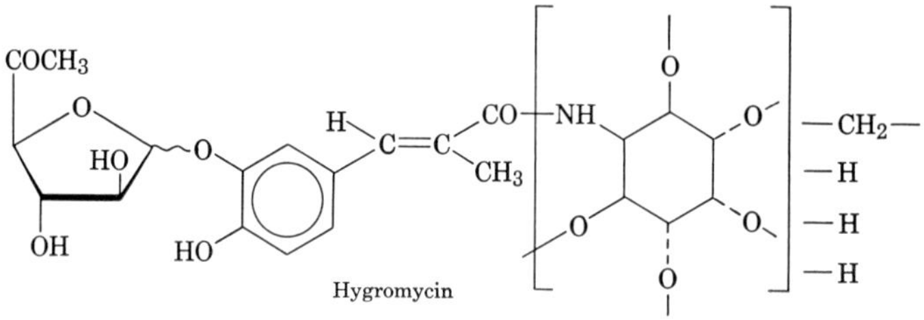

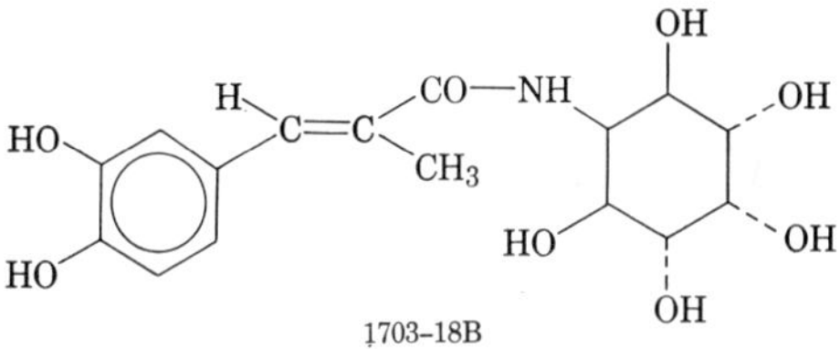

Fig. 5.20. Hygromycin, Mann and Woolf (M4); 1703-18B, Allen, Patrick, et al. (A6, P7).

mycin (M4) and the antibiotic 1703-18B (P7), and, indeed, the two antibiotics must be closely related since each contains the fragment shown in Fig. 5.20. Another antibiotic, homomycin, has been shown to contain a *neo*-inosamine fragment (N2).

OTHER AMINO SUGARS IN ANTIBIOTICS

In addition to the antibiotics that contain aminocyclitols as portions of their structure and that have been discussed above, many other antibiotics, less closely related, contain amino sugars. The structures of the more unusual amino

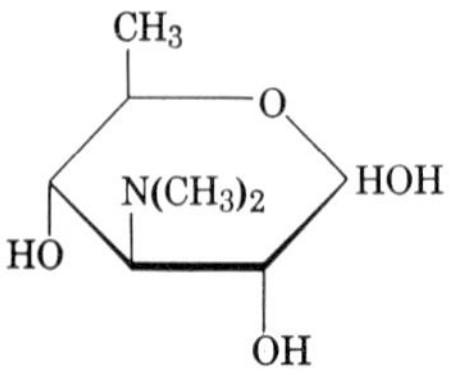

Mycaminose

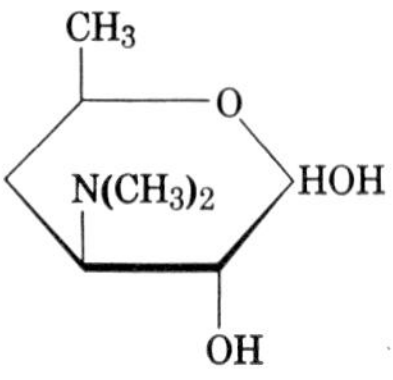

Desosamine

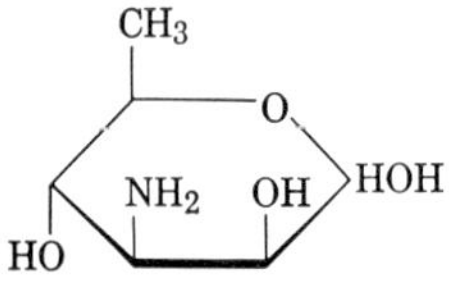

Mycosamine

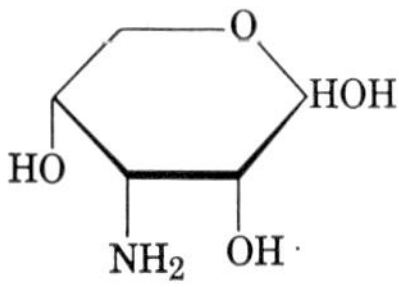

3-D-Ribosamine

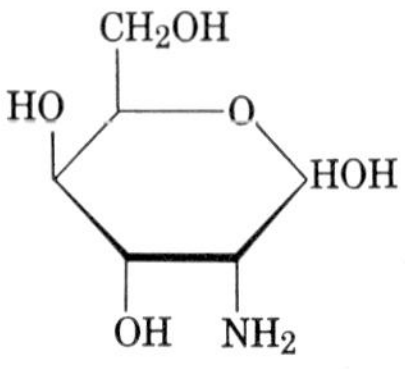

2-D-Gulosamine

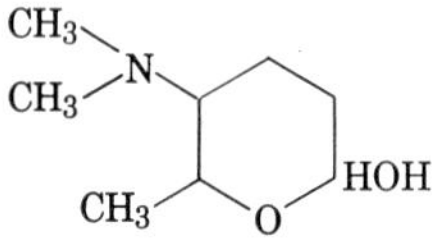

From spiramycin (P9)

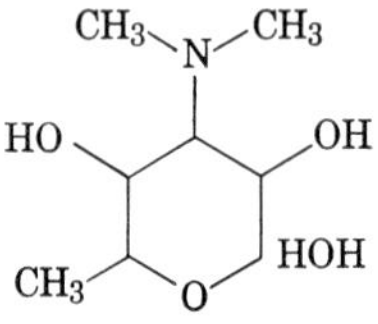

Amosamine

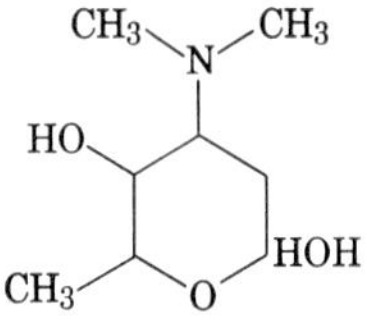

Rhodosamine

Fig. 5.21. Mycaminose (H16, R14, H18) has been obtained from magnamycins (H15), spiramycins (P8), and leucomycins (W10). Desosamine (H14, W9) has been obtained from erythromycins (F4), picromycin (B5), oleandomycin (E1), methymycins (D6, D7), narbomycin (C8), and griseomycin (V3). Mycosamine (V5) has been obtained from nystatin (W13), amphotericin B (W13), pimaricin (P10) and tetrins A and B (R19). 3-D-Ribosamine (W12) has been obtained from puromycin; 2-D-gulosamine (V2) from streptothricins and streptolins; amosamine (S13) from amicetin (S12); and rhodosamine (B4) from rhodomycin.

sugars thus far isolated from them are shown in Fig. 5.21. Stereochemistry is shown where it is known. Thus, mycosamine has D-mannose stereochemistry (V5), mycaminose (H18, R14) and desosamine (H14, W9) D-glucose stereochemistry. 3-Amino-D-ribose was isolated from puromycin (W12), and D-gulosamine from streptothricin and streptolin (V2). Trehalosamine, a streptomycete product of moderate antibiotic activity, is α-D-glucosido-α-D-glucosaminide (A3). Most of the macrolide and polyene antibiotics seem to contain amino sugar fragments as portions of their structures. The antibiotics from which the amino sugars have been obtained are indicated in the legend of Fig. 5.21.

ADDENDUM

Neomycins LP$_B$ and LP$_C$

Neomycins LP-I and LP-II have been shown (C12) to be mono-N-acetylated neomycins C and B, respectively, and have been renamed (C1) neomycins LP$_C$ and LP$_B$, accord-

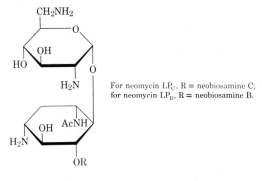

For neomycin LP$_C$, R = neobiosamine C; for neomycin LP$_B$, R = neobiosamine B.

Fig. 5.22. Chilton (C12, C13).

ingly. In each isomer the acetyl group is on the amino group of deoxystreptamine adjacent to the glycosidic link to neosamine C, as shown in Fig. 5.22. The structures were established by isolation of the same N-acetylneamine from each neomycin LP, reductive N-methylation of the N-acetyl-neamine and hydrolysis of the product to an N-methylated deoxystreptamine containing a free amino group. Perio-date evidence established the position of the N-acetyl group.

Paromomycin I Structure

Since the structure of neosamine B (paromose) is now certain (C12, R17, H19, R18) the structure assigned to paromomycin I (Fig. 5.6) is also certain.

Kanamycin A Structure

Nakabayashi (N4) has recently completed the assignment of absolute stereochemistry to deoxystreptamine in kana-mycin A, by the route shown in Fig. 5.23. Kanamycin A was hydrolyzed under mild acidic conditions to kanosami-nido-deoxystreptamine, whose components were identified by further hydrolysis. The tri-N-acetyl derivative of the intermediate disaccharide gave a strong positive increment in cuprammonium solution, establishing the absolute stereo-chemistry of the vicinal glycol.

Gentamicins C_1 and C_2

A fourth family of deoxystreptamine antibiotics has now been identified and named the gentamicin complex (W15). Surprisingly, these compounds are isolated from micro-organisms other than streptomycetes, from *Micromonospora purpurea n. sp.* and from *Micromonospora echinospora n. sp.*

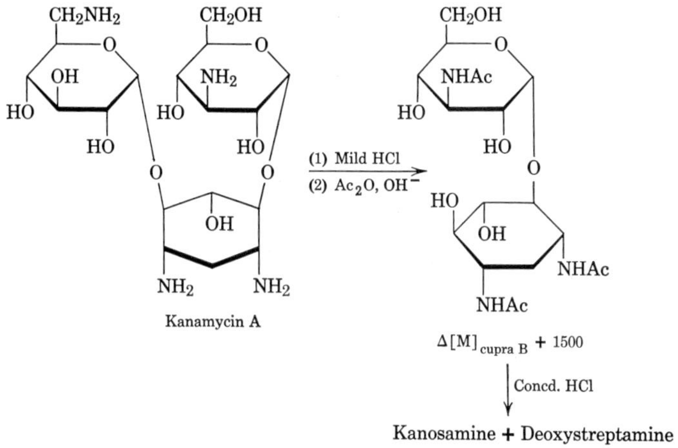

Fig. 5.23. Nakabayashi (N4).

Two members of the family have been described, genta-micins C_1 and C_2, which are apparently isomeric, with molecular formula $C_{17-18}H_{34-36}N_4O_7$. They have very simi-lar rotations and are stable to alkali. Each has three pri-mary amino groups, one N-methyl group and one C-methyl group, forms an N-triacetyl derivative, and gives deoxystrep-tamine on acidic hydrolysis. The properties described establish the gentamicins as a distinctly separate group of the deoxystreptamine family.

Bluensomycin Structure

The antibiotic bluensomycin, whose structure (Fig. 5.24) recently has been established by Bannister and Argoudelis (B6), provides a bridge between the streptomycin antibiotics and those containing an inosamine residue. It is very nearly a streptomycin: It contains dihydrostreptobiosamine, with

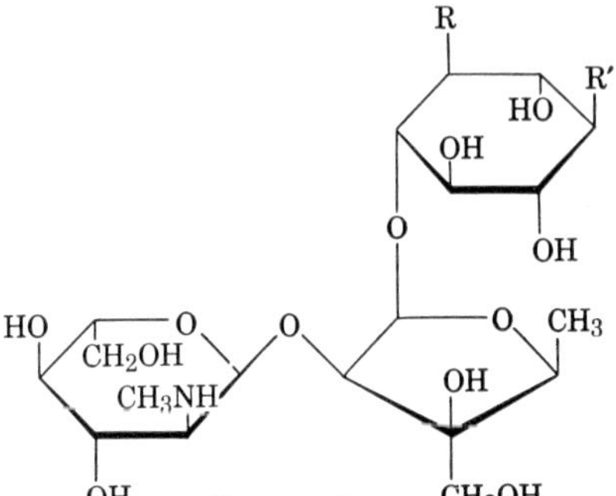

Fig. 5.24. Bannister and Argoudelis (B6, B7).

dihydrostreptose and N-methyl-L-glucosamine, but instead of streptidine, its third component, named bluensidine (B7), is a mono-guanido mono-carbamyl derivative of *scyllo*-inosamine.   The more likely structure on biogenetic grounds is the first:

$$R = -\text{NH}\overset{\text{NH}}{\overset{\|}{\text{C}}}\text{NH}_2$$

Amosamine Structure

Amosamine has now been assigned D-gluco stereochemistry (S14), as shown in Fig. 5.25.

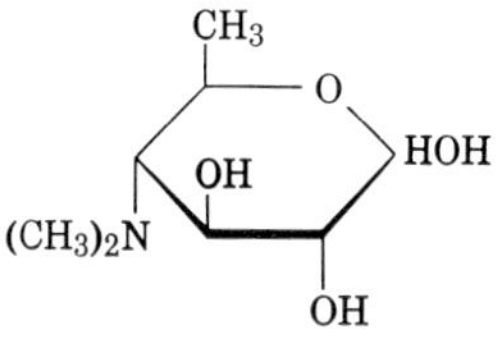

Fig. 5.25. Stevens, Blumbergs, and Daniher (S14).

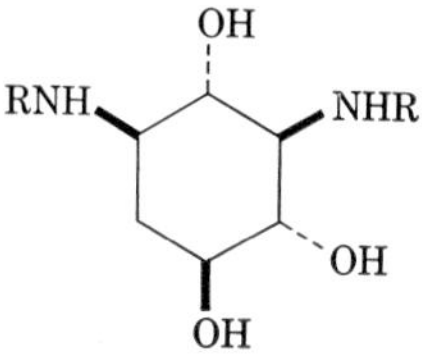

$R = Ac, \Delta[M]_{cupra\ B} = -2400°$

Fig. 5.26. Dyer and Todd (D9).

Streptomycin Structure

The absolute stereochemistry of streptidine in streptomycin (hence in dihydrostreptomycin, hydroxystreptomycin, and mannosidostreptomycin) has been determined by Dyer and Todd (D9) through application of Reeves' cuprammonium method. The method was discussed in Chapter 4 in its application to deoxystreptamine in the neomycins. In the streptidine study the requisite asymmetric diol was the di-N-acetyl derivative (R = Ac) shown in Fig. 5.26, which was obtained from the unsymmetrical di-N-benzoyl compound (R = ØCO) isolated earlier by the Merck group (K5). The configuration assigned is the same as that suggested by Tatsuoka and Horii (T3) from the rotation of N,N′-diacetyl-2,5,6-tri-O-methylstreptamine and later confirmed by the same authors (T4) by Reeves' method, applied to di-N-acetyl-2,6-di-O-methylstreptamine. The latter compound was obtained from dihydrostreptomycin by a sequence including partial O-methylation of the deguanylated, N-acetylated antibiotic.

6

BIOSYNTHETIC CONSIDERATIONS

CORRELATION OF STEREOCHEMISTRY

As has been noted earlier, neomycins B and C are exceedingly closely related, their structures differing only in the stereochemistry at a single asymmetric center. Other antibiotic mixtures are similarly closely related. The paromomycins (zygomycins A) apparently differ from one another in the same way that neomycin B differs from neomycin C—in the stereochemistry at one asymmetric center. Equally striking is the close relationship of the neomycins to the paromomycins, since neomycin B differs from paromomycin I only by the exchange of a single amino group by a hydroxyl group; and neomycin C and paromomycin II are similarly related. A like relationship (interchange of hydroxyl and amino groups) is found between kanamycins A and C and, perhaps, B. Thus these three groups of antibiotics are clearly related in their formation as well as in their structures.

Perhaps more striking still is the stereochemical similarity of the three diamino fragments from neomycin B—deoxystreptamine, neosamine C, and neosamine B. This is especially apparent if they are written in the form shown in

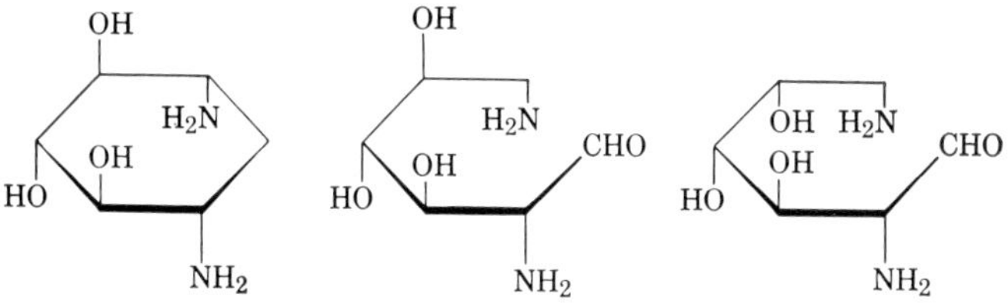

Deoxystreptamine   Neosamine B   Neosamine C

Fig. 6.1

Fig. 6.1, where it may be seen that the only position which differs stereochemically is C-5 of neosamine C.

Since the deoxystreptamine antibiotics are rather important compounds, it seems desirable to inquire as to their mode of formation in nature. Moreover, since they do consist of mixtures of very closely related isomers a biosynthetic scheme for one is presumably applicable to all. For these reasons it has been considered profitable to devise a hypothetical biogenetic scheme for the neomycins, and experimental work designed to test these hypotheses has begun.

SPECULATION

The initially proposed overall scheme is outlined in Fig. 6.2. In this scheme D-glucose is proposed to give a key intermediate, 5-keto-2,6-diamino-2,6-dideoxy-D-glucose, which then may undergo aldol cyclization to give a cyclohexane derivative. On reduction, the latter would yield deoxystreptamine, the most stable isomer, with all substituents equatorial. Alternatively, the 5-keto intermediate could be reduced to give neosamine B and neosamine C.

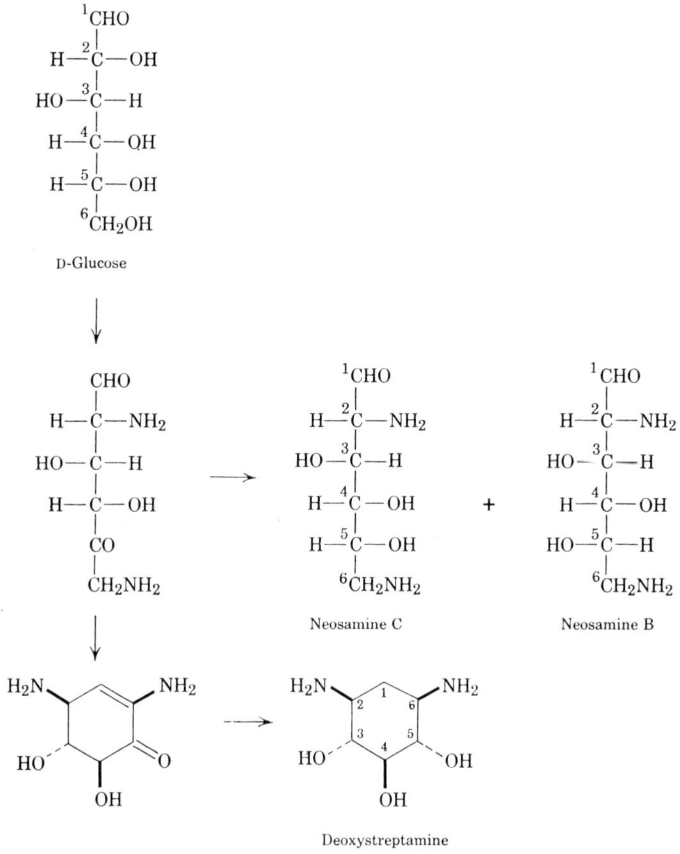

Fig. 6.2. Rinehart (R15).

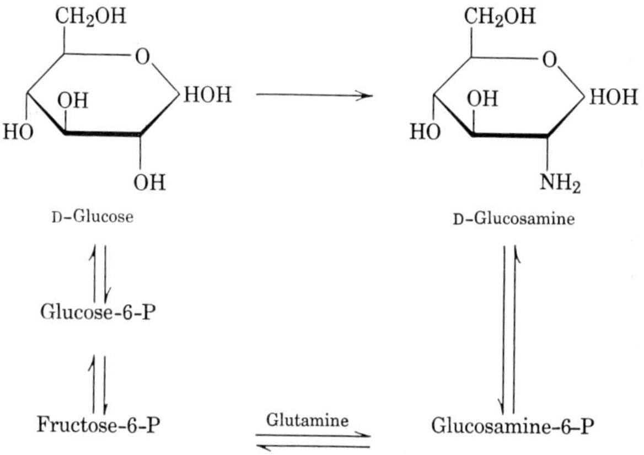

Fig. 6.3

More detailed consideration of the initial step in the sequence is presented in Fig. 6.3, where it is assumed that D-glucose goes initially to D-glucosamine. This step has been studied in a number of other laboratories (P11, K3), and it has been well authenticated that the carbon skeleton of glucose is not altered in this conversion and that the intermediates involved are probably D-fructose-6-phosphate and glucosamine-6-phosphate.

The next steps (shown in Fig. 6.4) involve conversion of D-glucosamine to the 5-ketodiaminohexose. This oxidation has not been demonstrated, but a number of analogous reactions are known. For example, *Acetobacter suboxydans* has been shown to produce 6-aldehydofructose (W14) and to convert N-acetyl-D-glucosaminol to 5-keto-N-acetyl-D-glucosaminol (J2). It may be noted, too, that a 5-keto sugar is found in the antibiotic hygromycin A (M4), which also contains the deoxystreptamine-like compound *neo*-inosa-

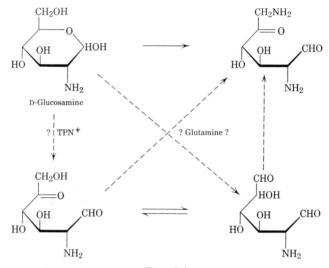

Fig. 6.4

mine (Fig. 5.20).   An alternative would involve conversion
to the 6-aldehydo compound rather than to the 5-keto; however, these two would be readily interconvertible.   At any
rate, amination in the 6-position would follow after the
formation of either the 5-keto or 6-aldehydo sugar, by a
mechanism analogous to that employed for the formation
of glucosamine from glucose.

The subsequent reduction step to neosamines B and C
would be, of course, quite easy.   In this connection it may
be noted that the occurrence of epimeric hexose derivatives
in the same source is well authenticated.   For example, it
has been demonstrated that UDP-N-acetylglucosamine may
be converted to UDP-N-acetylgalactosamine (F5), and UDP-

D-glucuronic acid to UDP-L-iduronic acid (N3); both of the latter are found in the chondroitin sulfates (H17). Interconversion of hexoses has recently been reviewed in a number of places [e.g. (R16)]. Perhaps the most striking example of such interconversions is the reported conversion of D-glucose to N-methyl-L-glucosamine (S9), in which the C-1 carbon of D-glucose becomes the C-1 carbon of N-methyl-L-glucosamine and every asymmetric center has been inverted.

The most novel step in the proposed biogenetic sequence, at least at the time of its first suggestion (R15), was the formation of deoxystreptamine directly from the diaminoketohexose. This was unusual, since earlier workers had reported that glucose is not converted intact to inositol (C11). The reverse sequence is well demonstrated, however, and each of the reactions involved is presumably reversible, so it was not unexpected when it was reported very recently that glucose is converted without rearrangement to inositol in parsley leaves (L8).

Beyond the diamino components of the neomycins, various biogenetic pathways exist for the conversion of D-glucose to the pentose fragment of the antibiotic, D-ribose. One of these is shown in Fig. 6.5. This is a well-authenticated sequence (F6) in which D-glucose is converted to D-glucose-6-phosphate to D-gluconolactone-6-phosphate to D-gluconic acid-6-phosphate. Presumably, an oxidation converts that compound to the 3-keto derivative and decarboxylation gives ribulose-6-phosphate, which on tautomerization gives ribose-6-phosphate and, ultimately, ribose-1-phosphate by way of ribose-1,6-diphosphate.

An alternative pathway to pentose from glucose (Fig. 6.6) might involve C-6 decarboxylation through an intermediate hexuronic acid (F7). Thus, a biogenetic scheme is avail-

```
      CHOH ─┐                        CO ─┐
   H ─ C ─ OH                     H ─ C ─ OH
  HO ─ C ─ H   O      ⇌          HO ─ C ─ H   O      +H₂O→
   H ─ C ─ OH         TPN⁺        H ─ C ─ OH          ←−H₂O
   H ─ C ─┘                       H ─ C ─┘
      CH₂OPO₃H₂                      CH₂OPO₃H₂
```

```
      COOH                    ┌      COOH      ┐
   H ─ C ─ OH                 │   H ─ C ─ OH   │
  HO ─ C ─ H      TPN⁺        │      CO         │     −CO₂
   H ─ C ─ OH      ⇌          │   H ─ C ─ OH   │      ───→
   H ─ C ─ OH                 │   H ─ C ─ OH   │
      CH₂OPO₃H₂               └      CH₂OPO₃H₂ ┘
```

```
      CH₂OH                    CHOH ─┐                 H   OPO₃H₂
      CO                    H ─ C ─ OH                  ＼C
   H ─ C ─ OH      ⇌        H ─ C ─ OH   O      ⇌     H ─ C ─ OH   O
   H ─ C ─ OH              H ─ C ─┘                   H ─ C ─ OH
      CH₂OPO₃H₂               CH₂OPO₃H₂               H ─ C ─┘
                                                         CH₂OH
```

Fig. 6.5

able for the formation of each of the four components of neomycin directly from glucose.

The individual components then could be joined together by the usual oligosaccharide route (F8), through their 1-phosphate derivatives (Fig. 6.7); presumably neosamine B-1-phosphate links to ribose and neosamine C-1-phosphate

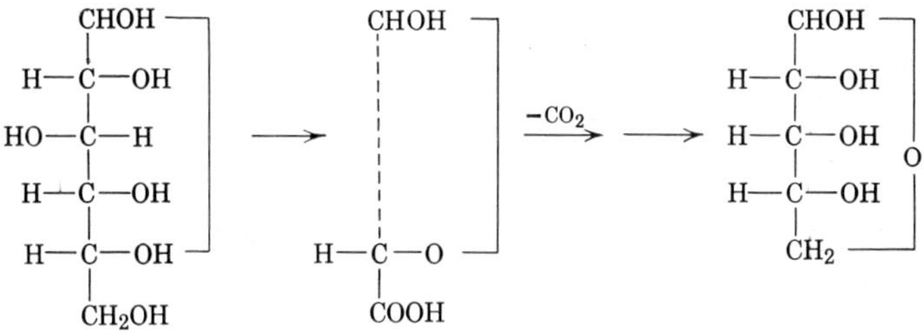

Fig. 6.6

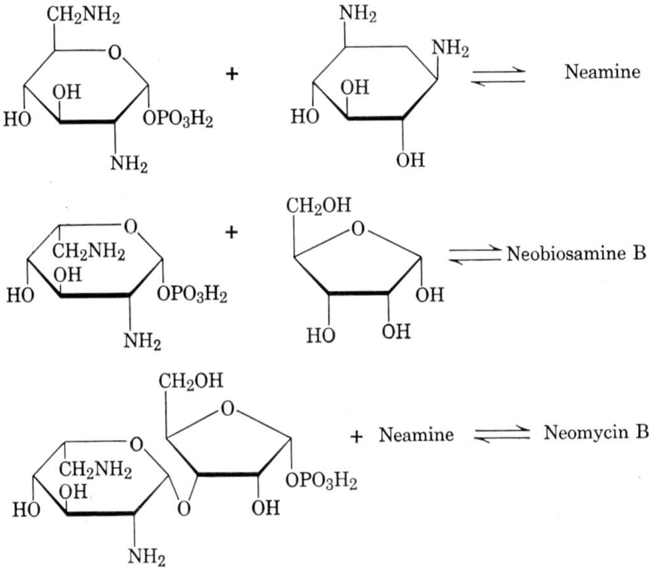

Fig. 6.7

to deoxystreptamine, to form neobiosamine B and neamine, respectively.   Neobiosamine B-1(ribose)-phosphate could then link to neamine.

It must be stressed that the discussion this far has presented only a hypothetical biogenesis.   It remained to submit this speculation to the sober eye of experiment.

BIOSYNTHETIC EXPERIMENTS

Evidence for the incorporation of glucose into neomycin was obtained quite early by Sebek, who showed that, with his strain of *Streptomyces fradiae,* nearly 20% of the uniformly labeled glucose fed was incorporated into neomycin (S4) from a complex medium.

Sebek's experiments have recently been repeated by Foght and Hichens (R2, R3), who have confirmed ready incorporation of glucose-14C into neomycin, though their incorporation was only about 4% rather than 19% (Table 6.1).   Approximately 67% of the D-glucose fed was expired as carbon dioxide, while 16% was found in the mycelium and an additional 13% was incorporated into apparently polymeric material, ninhydrin-positive, which did not move from the origin on paper chromatography.   No evidence is available on the nature of this material, but it could be a mucopolysaccharide related to the usual cell wall substituents.

The neomycin obtained from these experiments with uniformly labeled glucose was separated on charcoal into neomycin B and neomycin C, neomycin B was degraded, and each of its components was isolated.   The activities of these materials are indicated in Fig. 6.8.   One is struck initially by the similar level of activity in each of the four com-

TABLE 6.1

Fate of Labeled Precursors

Percent Incorporation into

Substrate	Neomycin	Mycelium	Brew	CO_2	Ref.
Glucose-U-^{14}C [a]	19.1	2.0	8.9	68.4	(S4)
-U-^{14}C	4.3	16.1	12.5	67.1	(R2, R3)
-1-^{14}C	4.3	22.0	10.0	63.6	(R2, R3)
Glucosamine-1-^{14}C	16.8	32.7	18.1	32.5	(R2, R3)
Neosamine B	23.8	9.7	52.3 [b]	14.2	(F9)
C	39.1	6.5	42.1 [c]	12.3	(F9)
Deoxystreptamine	52.3	5.0	19.8 [d]	22.9	(F9)

[a] Sebek, 1955.

[b] Includes 12.0% (of total) recovered precursor.

[c] Includes 7.0% precursor.

[d] Includes 9.8% precursor.

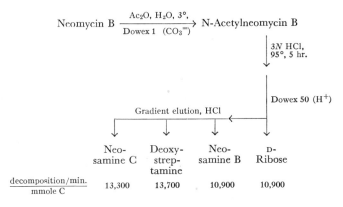

Fig. 6.8. Foght and Hichens (R2, R3).

ponents, which would be expected for a direct conversion of glucose to each component. This similarity seems to eliminate direct conversion to one component and complete breakdown and resynthesis of another component (e.g., ribose), though it does not eliminate complete resynthesis of *all* the components. It also may be noted that the four constituents of neomycin are grouped in pairs, with neosamine C and deoxystreptamine, the constituents of neamine, somewhat more active than ribose and neosamine B (the constituents of neobiosamine B).

Neomycin C from the run with uniformly labeled glucose was degraded in a similar fashion, though here the smaller quantities available did not allow isolation of the monosaccharides. Neobiosamine C was, surprisingly, more active than neamine, the reverse of the case with neomycin B (Fig. 6.9).

This experiment has been repeated with both glucose-1-^{14}C

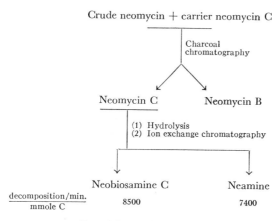

Fig. 6.9. Foght and Hichens (R2, R3).

TABLE 6.2

Incorporation of Glucose and Glucosamine into Neomycin Fragments

Relative Activity Level
(decomposition/min.)/mmole C

Substrate	Neo-samine C	Deoxy-strep-tamine	Neo-samine B	D-Ribose	Ref.
D-Glucose-U-^{14}C	0.97	1.00	0.80	0.80	(R2, R3)
-1-^{14}C	1.01	1.00	0.81	0.62	(R2, R3)
-6-^{14}C	0.98	1.00	0.79	0.31	(R2, R3)
D-Glucosamine-1-^{14}C	0.81	1.00	1.54	0.07	(R2, R3)
Neosamine B	0.46	1.00	0.22	0.13	(F9)
C	0.97	1.00	0.84	0.05	(F9)
Deoxystreptamine	0.09	1.00	0.04	0.03	(F9)

and glucose-6-^{14}C (R2, R3). The level of labeling of the three nitrogen-containing fragments is almost exactly the same as that from glucose-U-^{14}C, but the activity per carbon atom is lower for ribose (Table 6.2). These results suggest again a lack of degradation and resynthesis in the amino compounds. The ribose incorporation is most readily explained as arising from a combination of the two suggested pathways (Figs. 6.5 and 6.6), with the latter more important.

Similar feeding experiments (R2, R3) have been carried out with glucosamine-1-^{14}C (Tables 6.1 and 6.2). Two results are significant. First, the level of incorporation into neomycin is much higher with this precursor than with glucose. This establishes glucosamine as being further along the biosynthetic path and indirectly confirms the proposed first step (Fig. 6.3). Second, D-ribose is only very slightly labeled. This means glucosamine is not broken down to any great degree into metabolic pool intermediates but is converted rather rapidly to other compounds, which find their way into neomycin.

The high level of labeling from glucosamine-1-^{14}C allowed the isolated fragments—deoxystreptamine, neosamine B, and neosamine C—to be reintroduced into the growth medium (F9). Each of the three was reincorporated into neomycin B and the four monosaccharide fragments were reisolated (Tables 6.1 and 6.2). As expected, ribose was not labeled. Both neosamine B and neosamine C gave activity in all three diamino components, but active deoxystreptamine labeled neomycin B only in the deoxystreptamine fragment. Thus, the latter compound is apparently the terminal product of a reaction sequence and is not equilibrated with the other products and intermediates. All the above results can be summarized by the reaction scheme shown in Fig. 6.10.

Still in doubt is the nature of "X," which certainly consists of more than one step or intermediate. Whether C-1 of glucose or glucosamine remains C-1 of neosamine B or C or some more complex pattern is shown remains to be demonstrated, as does the labeling pattern in deoxystrepta-

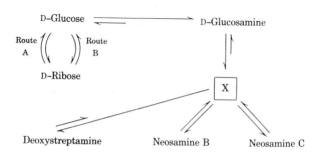

Fig. 6.10

mine.   The recent results cited, however, are in general
agreement with the biogenetic hypothesis and whet the
appetite for additional information.

In conclusion, then, it may be said that, while the structures of the neomycins are now established, interest in
these molecules is at least as strong as ever because of the
curious similarities of the compounds as established by
structural studies and the possible biogenetic implications
of these structures.   A great deal remains to be done.   The
entire area of biogenetic considerations deserves more ex-
tensive study, and some day one may wish to accept the
challenge of the total synthesis of the neomycins themselves.

ADDENDUM

The most recent experiments (S15) on the biosynthesis of
the neomycins have established that D-ribose-1-^{14}C is also
incorporated (6.4%) into the antibiotic. Unlike that of the
other subunits, however, ribose's activity is distributed
throughout the four fragments: 32% in ribose, 30% in
deoxystreptamine, 23% in neosamine C, and 15% in neosamine B.

The results with ribose indicate a rather high degree of
randomization of label with this precursor (although the
ribose isolated retains its label at C-1) and suggest more
randomization from the other precursors (especially glucose
and glucosamine) than earlier suspected.   This has been
confirmed (F9) by degradation of both of the neosamines
and deoxystreptamine from runs with labeled glucose (Fig.
6.11) and glucosamine (Fig. 6.12).   In each fragment some
retention of the label at its initial position was noted, but

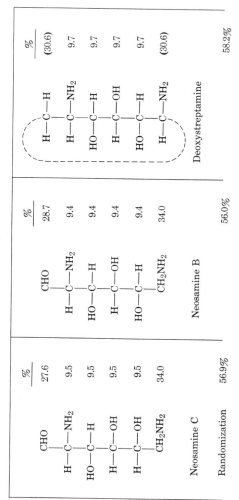

D-Glucose-1-^{14}C precursor

	%		%		%
CHO	27.6	CHO	28.7	H—C—H	(30.6)
H—C—NH$_2$	9.5	H—C—NH$_2$	9.4	H—C—NH$_2$	9.7
HO—C—H	9.5	HO—C—H	9.4	HO—C—H	9.7
H—C—OH	9.5	H—C—OH	9.4	H—C—OH	9.7
H—C—OH	9.5	HO—C—H	9.4	HO—C—H	9.7
CH$_2$NH$_2$	34.0	CH$_2$NH$_2$	34.0	H—C—NH$_2$	(30.6)
Neosamine C		Neosamine B		Deoxystreptamine	
Randomization	56.9%		56.0%		58.2%

Fig. 6.11. Foght (F9).

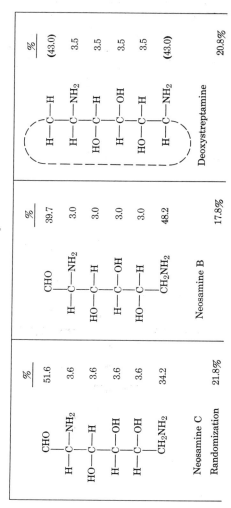

D-Glucosamine-1-^{14}C precursor

Fig. 6.12. Foght (F9).

considerable randomization was also evident (57% from glucose, 21% from glucosamine). An especially unexpected result is the near equivalence of C-1 and C-6 labeling, which could be explained either by a symmetrical intermediate (as in Fig. 6.13) or by a transaldolase-transketolase reaction path.

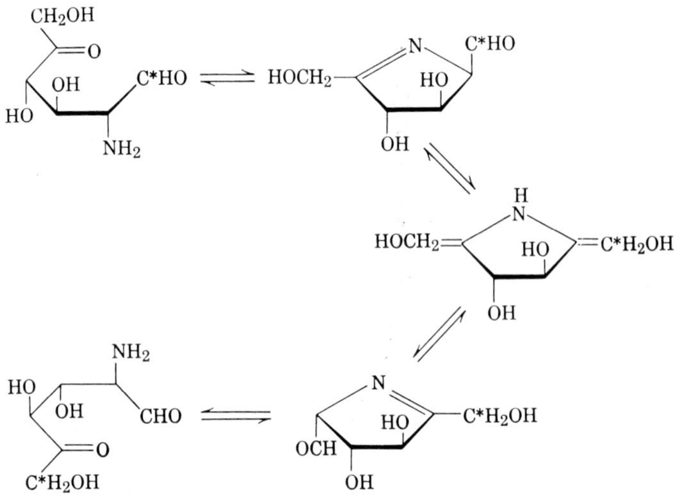

Fig. 6.13

REFERENCES

A1. S. J. Angyal and D. J. McHugh, *J. Chem. Soc.*, 1423 (1957).

A2. A. D. Argoudelis, unpublished results.

A3. F. Arcamone and F. Bizioli, *Gazz. Chim. Ital.*, **87**, 896 (1957).

A4. T. Arai, *J. Antibiotics (Tokyo), Ser. A*, **4**, 215 (1951).

A5. F. Arcamone, C. Bertazzoli, M. Ghione, and T. Scotti, *Giorn. Microbiol.*, **7**, 251 (1959).

A6. G. R. Allen, Jr., *J. Am. Chem. Soc.*, **78**, 5691 (1956).

B1. J. H. Brewster, *J. Am. Chem. Soc.*, **81**, 5475 (1959).

B2. G. R. Barker, T. M. Noone, D. C. C. Smith, and J. W. Spoors, *J. Chem. Soc.*, 1327 (1955).

B3. M. G. Brazhnikova, M. K. Kudinova, M. F. Lavrova, and T. A. Uspenskaya, *Antibiotiki*, **5**, No. 4, 6 (1960).

B4. H. Brockmann and E. Spohler, *Naturwissenschaften*, **42**, 154 (1955).

B5. H. Brockmann, *Angew. Chem.*, **65**, 257 (1953).

B6. B. Bannister and A. D. Argoudelis, *J. Am. Chem. Soc.*, **85**, 234 (1963).

B7. B. Bannister and A. D. Argoudelis, *J. Am. Chem. Soc.*, **85**, 119 (1963).

B8. T. F. Brodasky, *Anal. Chem.*, **35**, 343 (1963).

C1. W. S. Chilton, Ph.D. thesis, Univ. of Illinois, 1963.

C2. H. E. Carter, R. K. Clark, Jr., S. R. Dickman, Y. H. Loo, J. S. Meek, P. S. Skell, W. A. Strong, J. T. Alberi, Q. R. Bartz, S. B. Binkley, H. M. Crooks, Jr., I. R. Hooper, and M. C. Rebstock, *Science*, **103**, 53 (1946).

C3. H. E. Carter, J. R. Dyer, P. D. Shaw, K. L. Rinehart, Jr., and M. Hichens, *J. Am. Chem. Soc.,* **83,** 3723 (1961).

C4. H. E. Carter, R. K. Clark, Jr., S. R. Dickman, Y. H. Loo, P. S. Skell, and W. A. Strong, *Science,* **103,** 540 (1946).

C5. M. J. Cron, D. L. Evans, F. M. Palermiti, D. F. Whitehead, I. R. Hooper, P. Chu, and R. U. Lemieux, *J. Am. Chem. Soc.,* **80,** 4741 (1958).

C6. M. J. Cron, O. B. Fardig, D. L. Johnson, D. F. Whitehead, I. R. Hooper, and R. U. Lemieux, *J. Am. Chem. Soc.,* **80,** 4115 (1958).

C7. M. J. Cron, O. B. Fardig, D. L. Johnson, H. Schmitz, D. F. Whitehead, I. R. Hooper, and R. U. Lemieux, *J. Am. Chem. Soc.,* **80,** 2342 (1958).

C8. R. Corbaz, L. Ettlinger, E. Gäumann, W. Keller, F. Kradolfer, E. Kyburz, L. Neipp, V. Prelog, R. Reusser, and H. Zähner, *Helv. Chim. Acta,* **38,** 935 (1955).

C9. L. D. Colebrook and R. H. Gourlay, *Proc. Natl. Acad. Sci. U.S.,* **48,** 1693 (1962).

C10. D. D. Chapman, R. L. Autrey, R. H. Gourlay, A. L. Johnson, J. Souto, and D. S. Tarbell, *Proc. Natl. Acad. Sci. U.S.,* **48,** 1108 (1962).

C11. F. C. Charalampous, *J. Biol. Chem.,* **225,** 595 (1957).

C12. W. S. Chilton and K. L. Rinehart, Jr., 144th Mtg., Am. Chem. Soc., Los Angeles, Mar. 31–Apr. 5, 1963; see *Abstracts,* p. 42M.

D1. J. D. Dutcher, N. Hosansky, M. N. Donin, and O. Wintersteiner, *J. Am. Chem. Soc.,* **73,** 1384 (1951).

D2. J. D. Dutcher and M. N. Donin, *J. Am. Chem. Soc.,* **74,** 3420 (1952).

D3. J. R. Dyer, Ph.D. thesis, Univ. of Illinois, 1954.

D4. J. R. Dyer, *Methods Biochem. Analy.,* **3,** 111 (1956).

D5. J. W. Davisson, I. A. Solomons, and T. M. Lees, *Antibiot. Chemotherapy,* **2,** 460 (1952).

D6. C. Djerassi and J. A. Zderic, *J. Am. Chem. Soc.,* **78,** 6390 (1956).

D7. C. Djerassi and O. Halpern, *J. Am. Chem. Soc.,* **79,** 2022 (1957).

D8. J. D. Dutcher, in *Neomycin, Its Nature and Practical Application,* S. A. Waksman, ed., Williams and Wilkins Co., Baltimore, 1958, p. 75.

D9. J. R. Dyer and A. W. Todd, *J. Am. Chem. Soc.,* **85,** 3896 (1963).

E1. H. Els, W. D. Celmer, and K. Murai, *J. Am. Chem. Soc.*, **80**, 3777 (1958).

F1. J. H. Ford, M. E. Bergy, A. A. Brooks, E. R. Garrett, J. Alberti, J. R. Dyer, and H. E. Carter, *J. Am. Chem. Soc.*, **77**, 5311 (1955).

F2. A. B. Foster, *Advan. Carbohydrate Chem.*, **12**, 81 (1957).

F3. R. P. Frohardt, T. H. Haskell, J. Ehrlich, and M. P. Knudsen, Belgian Pat. 547,976 (Oct. 12, 1956, to Parke, Davis and Co.); see *Chem. Zentr.*, **129**, 14128 (1958); **131**, 15843 (1960).

F4. E. H. Flynn, M. V. Sigal, P. F. Wiley, and K. Gerzon, *J. Am. Chem. Soc.*, **76**, 3121 (1954).

F5. J. S. Fruton and S. Simmonds, *General Biochemistry*, 2nd ed., John Wiley and Sons, New York, 1958, p. 464.

F6. *Ibid.*, pp. 313 and 526.

F7. *Ibid.*, p. 538.

F8. *Ibid.*, p. 446.

F9. J. L. Foght, Ph.D. thesis, Univ. of Illinois, 1963.

H1. Reviewed by J. E. Hawkins, Jr., in *Neomycin, Its Nature and Practical Application*, S. A. Waksman, ed., Williams and Wilkins Co., Baltimore, 1958, Chapter 11.

H2. M. Hichens and K. L. Rinehart, Jr., *J. Am. Chem. Soc.*, **85**, 1547 (1963).

H3. H. Hoeksema, A. D. Argoudelis, and P. F. Wiley, *J. Am. Chem. Soc.*, **84**, 3212 (1962).

H4. T. H. Haskell, J. C. French, and Q. R. Bartz, *J. Am. Chem. Soc.*, **81**, 3482 (1959).

H5. T. H. Haskell, J. C. French, and Q. R. Bartz, *J. Am. Chem. Soc.*, **81**, 3480 (1959).

H6. T. H. Haskell, J. C. French, and Q. R. Bartz, *J. Am. Chem. Soc.*, **81**, 3481 (1959).

H7. T. H. Haskell, personal communication.

H8. M. Hichens, unpublished results.

H9. S. Horii, *J. Antibiotics (Tokyo)*, Ser. *A*, **14**, 249 (1961).

H10. G. Hagemann, F. Nominé, and L. Penasse, *Ann. Pharm. Franc.*, **16**, 585 (1958).

H11. S. Horii, *J. Antibiotics (Tokyo)*, Ser. *A*, **15**, 187 (1962).

H12. I. R. Hooper, personal communication.

H13. H. Hitomi, S. Horii, T. Yamaguchi, M. Imanishi, and A. Miyake, *J. Antibiotics (Tokyo), Ser. A*, **14**, 63 (1961).

H14. W. Hofheinz and H. Grisebach, *Tetrahedron Letters*, 377 (1962).

H15. F. A. Hochstein and K. Murai, *J. Am. Chem. Soc.*, **76**, 5080 (1954).

H16. F. A. Hochstein and P. P. Regna, *J. Am. Chem. Soc.*, **77**, 3353 (1955).

H17. P. Hoffman, A. Linker, and K. Meyer, *Science*, **124**, 1252 (1956).

H18. W. Hofheinz and H. Grisebach, *Z. Naturforsch.*, **17b**, 355 (1962).

H19. T. H. Haskell and S. Hanessian, 144th Mtg., Am. Chem Soc., Los Angeles, Mar. 31–Apr. 5, 1963; see *Abstracts*, p. 19C.

H20. S. Horii, H. Hitomi, and A. Miyake, *J. Antibiotics (Tokyo), Ser. A.*, **16**, 144 (1963).

J1. C. D. Jardetzky, *J. Am. Chem. Soc.*, **84**, 62 (1962).

J2. J. K. N. Jones, M. B. Perry, and J. C. Turner, *Can. J. Chem.*, **39**, 965 (1961).

K1. F. A. Kuehl, Jr., M. N. Bishop, and K. Folkers, *J. Am. Chem. Soc.*, **73**, 881 (1951).

K2. For a review, see P. W. Kent and M. W. Whitehouse, *Biochemistry of the Aminosugars*, Butterworths Publications, London, 1955, p. 235.

K3. *Ibid.*, p. 27.

K4. R. Kuhn, W. Bister, and H. Fischer, *Ann. Chem.*, **617**, 109 (1958).

K5. F. A. Kuehl, Jr., R. L. Peck, C. E. Hoffhine, Jr., and K. Folkers, *J. Am. Chem. Soc.*, **70**, 2325 (1948).

L1. Reviewed by C. S. Livingood and E. Shapiro, in *Neomycin, Its Nature and Practical Application*, S. A. Waksman, ed., Williams and Wilkins Co., Baltimore, 1958, Chapter 19.

L2. B. E. Leach and C. M. Teeters, *J. Am. Chem. Soc.*, **73**, 2794 (1951).

L3. B. E. Leach and C. M. Teeters, *J. Am. Chem. Soc.*, **74**, 3187 (1952).

L4. R. U. Lemieux and R. J. Cushley, *Can. J. Chem.*, **41**, 858 (1963).

L5. R. U. Lemieux, R. K. Kullnig, and R. Y. Moir, *J. Am. Chem. Soc.*, **80**, 2237 (1958).

L6. H. A. Lechevalier, in *Neomycin, Its Nature and Practical Application*, S. A. Waksman, ed., Williams and Wilkins Co., Baltimore, 1958, p. 42.

L7. R. U. Lemieux and M. L. Wolfrom, *Advan. Carbohydrate Chem.,* **3,** 337 (1948).

L8. F. A. Loewus and S. Kelly, *Biochem. Biophys. Res. Commun.,* **7,** 204 (1962).

M1. Reviewed by L. S. Mann, in *Neomycin, Its Nature and Practical Application,* S. A. Waksman, ed., Williams and Wilkins Co., Baltimore, 1958, Chapter 21.

M2. K. Maeda, *J. Antibiotics (Tokyo), Ser. A,* **5,** 343 (1952).

M3. K. Maeda, M. Murase, H. Mawatari, and H. Umezawa, *J. Antibiotics (Tokyo), Ser. A,* **11,** 163 (1958).

M4. R. L. Mann and D. O. Woolf, *J. Am. Chem. Soc.,* **79,** 120 (1957).

M5. K. Maeda, M. Murase, H. Mawatari, and H. Umezawa, *J. Antibiotics (Tokyo), Ser. A,* **11,** 163 (1958).

M6. M. W. Miller, *Pfizer Handbook of Microbial Metabolites,* McGraw-Hill Book Co., New York, 1961.

M7. M. Murase, *J. Antibiotics (Tokyo), Ser. A,* **14,** 367 (1961).

M8. H. Maehr and C. P. Schaffner, *Anal. Chem.,* **36,** in press (1964).

N1. M. Namiki, K. Isono, K. Anzai, and S. Suzuki, *J. Antibiotics (Tokyo), Ser. A,* **10,** 160 (1957).

N2. M. Namiki, K. Isono, K. Anzai, and S. Suzuki, *J. Antibiotics (Tokyo), Ser. A,* **10,** 170 (1957).

N3. E. F. Neufeld, 140th National Meeting, American Chemical Society, Chicago, Sept. 1961; see *Abstracts,* p. 10D.

N4. T. Nakabayashi and K. L. Rinehart, Jr., unpublished results.

O1. H. Ogawa and T. Ito, *J. Antibiotics (Tokyo), Ser. A,* **10,** 267 (1957).

O2. H. Ogawa, T. Ito, S. Inoue, and S. Kondo, *J. Antibiotics (Tokyo), Ser. A,* **11,** 70 (1958).

O3. H. Ogawa, T. Ito, S. Inoue, and S. Kondo, *J. Antibiotics (Tokyo), Ser. A,* **11,** 72, 166 (1958).

O4. H. Ohle and L. v. Vargha, *Ber.,* **61,** 1203 (1928).

P1. S. C. Pan and J. D. Dutcher, *Anal. Chem.,* **28,** 836 (1956).

P2. R. L. Peck, C. E. Hoffhine, Jr., P. Gale, and K. Folkers, *J. Am. Chem. Soc.,* **71,** 2590 (1949).

P3. D. Perlman and E. O'Brien, *Bacteriol. Proc. (Soc. Am. Bacteriologists),* **1953,** 20.

P4. R. L. Peck, C. E. Hoffhine, Jr., E. W. Peel, R. P. Graber, F. W.

Holly, R. Mozingo, and K. Folkers, *J. Am. Chem. Soc.*, **68**, 776 (1946).

P5. J. A. Pople, W. G. Schneider, and H. J. Bernstein, *High-Resolution Nuclear Magnetic Resonance*, McGraw-Hill Book Co., New York, 1959, p. 397.

P6. S. Peat and L. F. Wiggins, *J. Chem. Soc.*, 1810 (1938).

P7. J. B. Patrick, R. P. Williams, C. W. Waller, and B. L. Hutchings, *J. Am. Chem. Soc.*, **78**, 2652 (1956).

P8. R. Paul and S. Tchelitcheff, *Bull. soc. chim. France*, 1059 (1957).

P9. R. Paul and S. Tchelitcheff, *Bull. soc. chim. France*, 734 (1957).

P10. J. B. Patrick, R. P. Williams, and J. S. Webb, *J. Am. Chem. Soc.*, **80**, 6689 (1958).

P11. B. M. Pogell and R. M. Gryder, *J. Biol. Chem.*, **228**, 701 (1957).

R1. K. L. Rinehart, Jr., A. D. Argoudelis, W. A. Goss, A. Sohler, and C. P. Schaffner, *J. Am. Chem. Soc.*, **82**, 3938 (1960).

R2. K. L. Rinehart, Jr., M. Hichens, and J. L. Foght, *Ind. Chim. Belge*, **27**, 552 (1962).

R3. K. L. Rinehart, Jr., M. Hichens, and J. L. Foght, 142nd National Meeting, American Chemical Society, Atlantic City, Sept. 9–14, 1962; see *Abstracts*, p. 4P.

R4. K. L. Rinehart, Jr., P. W. K. Woo, A. D. Argoudelis, and A. M. Giesbrecht, *J. Am. Chem. Soc.*, **79**, 4567 (1957).

R5. K. L. Rinehart, Jr., and P. W. K. Woo, *J. Am. Chem. Soc.*, **83**, 643 (1961).

R6. K. L. Rinehart, Jr., P. W. K. Woo, and A. D. Argoudelis, *J. Am. Chem. Soc.*, **80**, 6461 (1958).

R7. K. L. Rinehart, Jr., P. W. K. Woo, and A. D. Argoudelis, *J. Am. Chem. Soc.*, **79**, 4568 (1957).

R8. K. L. Rinehart, Jr., and P. W. K. Woo, *J. Am. Chem. Soc.*, **80**, 6463 (1958).

R9. K. L. Rinehart, Jr., M. Hichens, A. D. Argoudelis, W. S. Chilton, H. E. Carter, M. Georgiadis, C. P. Schaffner, and R. T. Schillings, *J. Am. Chem. Soc.*, **84**, 3218 (1962).

R10. K. L. Rinehart, Jr., M. Hichens, K. Striegler, K. R. Rover, T. P. Culbertson, S. Tatsuoka, S. Horii, T. Yamaguchi, H. Hitomi, and A. Miyake, *J. Am. Chem. Soc.*, **83**, 2964 (1961).

R11. K. L. Rinehart, Jr., W. S. Chilton, and W. v. Phillipsborn, *J. Am. Chem. Soc.*, **84**, 3216 (1962).

R12. K. L. Rinehart, Jr., A. D. Argoudelis, T. P. Culbertson, W. S. Chilton, and K. Striegler, *J. Am. Chem. Soc.*, **82**, 2970 (1960).

R13. R. E. Reeves, *Advan. Carbohydrate Chem.*, **6**, 107 (1951).

R14. A. C. Richardson, *Proc. Chem. Soc.*, 430 (1961).

R15. K. L. Rinehart, Jr., Abstracts of 17th National Organic Symposium, Bloomington, Ind., June, 1961, p. 96.

R16. S. Roseman, *Federation Proc.*, **18**, 984 (1959).

R17. K. L. Rinehart, Jr., Conference on Structural Organic Chemistry, Quartermaster Research and Engineering Command, Natick, Mass., Oct. 18–19, 1962.

R18. W. M. z. Reckendorf, *Angew. Chem.*, **74**, 573 (1963).

R19. K. L. Rinehart, Jr., V. F. German, W. P. Tucker, and D. Gottlieb, *Ann. Chem.*, **668**, 77 (1963).

R20. K. L. Rinehart, Jr., M. Hichens, and W. S. Chilton, 2nd International Symposium on the Chemistry of Organic Natural Products, Prague, Aug. 27–Sept. 2, 1963; see G. Fodor, *Chem. Ind. (London)*, 1856 (1962).

R21. K. L. Rinehart, Jr., M. Hichens, J. L. Foght, and W. S. Chilton, *Antimicrobial Agents and Chemotherapy*, **1962**, 193.

S1. E. A. Swart, D. Hutchison, and S. A. Waksman, *Arch. Biochem.*, **24**, 92 (1949).

S2. E. A. Swart, H. A. Lechevalier, and S. A. Waksman, *J. Am. Chem. Soc.*, **73**, 3253 (1951).

S3. C. P. Schaffner, *Antibiot. Ann.*, **1954–1955**, 153.

S4. O. K. Sebek, *J. Bacteriol.*, **75**, 199 (1958).

S5. G. Slomp and F. A. MacKellar, *Tetrahedron Letters*, 521 (1962).

S6. H. Straube-Rieke, H. A. Lardy, and L. Anderson, *J. Am. Chem. Soc.*, **75**, 694 (1953).

S7. M. M. Shemyakin, A. S. Khokhlov, M. N. Kolosov, L. D. Bergelson, and V. K. Antonov, *Khimiya Antibiotikov*, 3rd ed., Moscow, 1961.

S8. R. T. Schillings and C. P. Schaffner, *Antimicrobial Agents and Chemotherapy*, **1961**, 274.

S9. M. Silverman and S. V. Rieder, *J. Biol. Chem.*, **235**, 1251 (1960).

S10. E. A. Swart, A. H. Romano, and S. A. Waksman, *Proc. Soc. Exptl. Biol. Med.*, **73**, 376 (1950).

S11. H. Schmitz, O. B. Fardig, F. A. O'Herron, M. A. Rousche, and I. R. Hooper, *J. Am. Chem. Soc.*, **80**, 2911 (1958).

S12. C. L. Stevens, R. J. Gasser, T. K. Mukherjee, and T. H. Haskell, *J. Am. Chem. Soc.*, **78**, 6212 (1956).

S13. C. L. Stevens, K. Nagarajan, and T. H. Haskell, *J. Org. Chem.*, **27**, 2991 (1962).

S14. C. L. Stevens, P. Blumbergs, and F. A. Daniher, *J. Am. Chem. Soc.*, **85**, 1552 (1963).

S15. R. F. Schimbor and K. L. Rinehart, Jr., unpublished results.

T1. T. Takeuchi, T. Hikiji, K. Nitta, S. Yamazuki, S. Abe, H. Takayama, and H. Umezawa, *J. Antibiotics (Tokyo), Ser. A,* **10,** 107 (1957).

T2. S. Tatsuoka, A. Miyake, and H. Nawa, *J. Antibiotics (Tokyo), Ser. A,* **11,** 193 (1958).

T3. S. Tatsuoka and S. Horii, *Proc. Japan Acad.,* **39,** 314 (1963).

T4. S. Tatsuoka, S. Horii, T. Yamaguchi, H. Hitomi, and A. Miyake, *Antimicrobial Agents and Chemotherapy,* **1962,** 188.

T5. S. Tatsuoka and S. Horii, personal communication.

U1. S. Umezawa, Y. Ito, and S. Fukatsu, *J. Antibiotics (Tokyo), Ser. A,* **11,** 162 (1958).

V1. E. E. Van Tamelen, *Fortschr. Chem. org. Naturstoffe,* **16,** 124 (1958).

V2. E. E. Van Tamelen, J. R. Dyer, H. E. Carter, J. V. Pierce, and E. E. Daniels, *J. Am. Chem. Soc.*, **78**, 4817 (1956).

V3. P. J. Van Dijck, H. P. Van de Voorde, and P. De Somer, *Antibiot. Chemotherapy,* **3,** 1243 (1953).

V4. D. Van Stolk, L. Mester, and M.-M. Janot, personal communication.

V5. M. H. Von Saltza, J. Reid, J. D. Dutcher, and O. Wintersteiner, *J. Am. Chem. Soc.*, **83**, 2785 (1961).

W1. S. A. Waksman and H. A. Lechevalier, *Science,* **109,** 305 (1949).

W2. O. Wintersteiner and A. Klingsberg, *J. Am. Chem. Soc.*, **70**, 885 (1948).

W3. M. L. Wolfrom, S. M. Olin, and W. J. Polglase, *J. Am. Chem. Soc.*, **72**, 1724 (1950).

W4. H. Weidmann and H. K. Zimmerman, Jr., *Angew. Chem.*, **72**, 750 (1960).

W5. O. Wintersteiner and A. Klingsberg, *J. Am. Chem. Soc.,* **73,** 2917 (1951).

W6. S. A. Waksman, ed., *Streptomycin,* Williams and Wilkins Co., Baltimore, 1949.

W7. S. A. Waksman, *Antibiot. Chemotherapy,* **3,** 333 (1953).

W8. P. F. Wiley, *J. Am. Chem. Soc.,* **84,** 1514 (1962).

W9. P. W. K. Woo, H. W. Dion, L. Durham, and H. S. Mosher, *Tetrahedron Letters,* 735 (1962).

W10. T. Watanabe, *Bull. Chem. Soc. Japan,* **34,** 15 (1961).

W11. T. Wakazawa and S. Fukatsu, *J. Antibiotics (Tokyo), Ser. A,* **15,** 225 (1962).

W12. C. W. Waller, P. W. Fryth, B. L. Hutchings, and J. H. Williams, *J. Am. Chem. Soc.,* **75,** 2025 (1953).

W13. D. R. Walters, J. D. Dutcher, and O. Wintersteiner, *J. Am. Chem. Soc.,* **79,** 5076 (1957).

W14. R. Weidenhagen and G. Bernsee, *Angew. Chem.,* **72,** 109 (1960).

W15. M. J. Weinstein, G. M. Luedemann, E. M. Oden, G. H. Wagman, J. P. Rosselet, J. Marquez, C. T. Coniglio, W. Charney, H. Herzog, and J. Black, *J. Med. Chem.,* **6,** 463 (1963).

INDEX

125